THE GANGSTER'S GUIDE TO SOBRIETY

THE GANGSTER'S GUIDE TO SOBRIETY

MY LIFE IN

12 STEPS

RICHIE STEPHENS
with JOHN ALTSCHULER and DAVE KRINSKY

Post Hill
PRESS

A POST HILL PRESS BOOK
ISBN: 978-1-63758-190-2
ISBN (eBook): 978-1-63758-188-9

The Gangster's Guide to Sobriety:
My Life in 12 Steps
© 2022 by Richie Stephens with John Altschuler and Dave Krinsky
All Rights Reserved

Cover design by Donna McLeer

Post Hill Press
New York • Nashville
posthillpress.com

Published in the United States of America
1 2 3 4 5 6 7 8 9 10

To Bernard
Thank you for saving my life.

TABLE OF CONTENTS

FOREWORD

I STILL DON'T KNOW WHY I didn't hit delete. An email sat in my inbox from someone I did not know. That means delete the message and mark it as spam. My writing partner, Dave Krinsky, and I have had some success with *King of the Hill*, *Blades of Glory*, and *Silicon Valley*, so we get a lot of projects sent to us from just about everywhere. Our lawyer has always been very clear: "DELETE!!! Do not even read the email. That could open you up to a lawsuit!" So, with a severe lack of judiciousness, I opened and read the email.

It was from someone named Richie Stephens, who made it clear he was legitimate by including his IMDb page, which showed he was a working actor. An actor—wonderful. But I kept reading, and his email was so straightforward and polite that I found it engaging. He wanted me to meet with him to talk about the business. Could we meet for coffee to discuss? Obviously not...right?

Well, there I am the next day at Starbucks, sitting across from this blond, rugged-looking guy. As handsome as you can look with a clearly broken and poorly set nose. This was Richie Stephens.

I had talked Dave into coming. For some reason, I figured Dave needed to witness this fiasco as well. So, there we were, listening to Richie. Not just listening, but hanging on his every word. Part of that might have been because he's Irish—not of Irish descent, but off-the-boat Irish. He kept calling me and Dave "Mush," and we had to ask him to repeat things that we just couldn't understand.

As we talked, intriguing pieces of information kept falling—"Before I was sober," "When I was a dealer," "When I quit being a gangster to get sober." Okay, this conversation was getting very interesting...especially when Richie said, "Of course, when you are a drug addict you obviously want the best drugs, and the best drugs were sold by an Asian gang in San Francisco...so I moved there from Ireland. And when I couldn't afford to buy all the drugs I was using, I joined their gang so I could deal them and keep enough for myself. Now, it was an all-Asian gang...well, until they had me."

Then, off-handedly, he mentioned that he had lost his mind to drugs and alcohol and nearly committed suicide before getting sober and moving to LA to become an actor. The last part was the saddest part of the story to Dave and me. There is nothing harder than being a struggling actor. He understood the irony of that as well. He had a comic understanding about how surreal his life was, and a pleasant sense of gratitude for having survived to tell the tale.

Still, I could not figure out why I was not hitting delete. I am leery of drug addicts and alcoholics because they don't go down without dragging everybody around along with them. And I find their rationalizations tedious. But Richie was sober. When I asked, "How long?" he replied, "Just a bit shy of nine years." This gave me pause; my wife is a psychologist and has told me that until an addict is sober a solid ten years, you can't trust them. But there he was, laughing about something that his kids had done and talking about his need to stay sober and help others find their way out of the morass of drugs and alcohol that had consumed him.

I looked over to Dave, who literally just nodded. We were both in. Richie did not even know that we had decided that his story had to be told. So, we never hit delete. I have no idea why. I ask Dave, and he just shrugs. Sometimes things don't make sense and cannot be explained, but, if you follow your heart, you end up where you need to be. That is what Richie's story is all about.

—JOHN ALTSCHULER

STEP ONE

IT ALL MADE SENSE
AT THE TIME

---※---

ADMIT YOU ARE POWERLESS OVER
DRUGS AND ALCOHOL,
AND THAT YOUR LIFE HAS BECOME
UNMANAGEABLE

---※---

I HAD MY FIRST DRINK in 1998 at the age of fifteen. I had my last one (hopefully) on August 31, 2010, when I was twenty-eight. In between were countless steps, missteps, stumbles, and face-plants, from backstreet pubs in Ireland to Hollywood parties to whorehouses in Australia to too many other fucked-up places in between to count or remember. Booze and drugs got me ass-kickings, trips to jails and hospitals, and cost me a shitload of friends and lovers. But, oh, that first drink was something special.

It was a wet Irish summer day, and I was on a bus coming back from "The Big Day Out," one of those festival-type concerts. Pulp was the headliner, and the bill included the Beastie Boys, Garbage, Cornershop, and Ian Brown from The Stone Roses. While I don't remember much about the performances, I remember well the girl who gave me my first drink—Aoife.

Aoife went to the same primary school as me. Her parents were rich; they owned a factory in town and had airs and graces. They even had their own private plane. Maybe all this money and privilege is what made Aoife such a rebel; she was well known as a drinker and cigarette smoker.

I wasn't known for much of anything. I was just a good quiet boy, tall and skinny. Even though I was an athlete, I was barely on a team. Even though I was in the top class at school, my report card always said, "Can do better." I was about as average as the Republic of Ireland could muster in the nineties—shy and well behaved, Mass every week, seldom stepped out of line.

But when Aoife passed that can of warm Heineken, I took it.

I remember thinking, *I want to be cool. I better not say no to this.*

Dara Slacke, my best friend at the time, looked at me disapprovingly. If I was right down the middle, Dara moved the needle pretty far into the nerdy range. This wasn't going to be *his* first drink, no way. I turned away and took a swig.

Wow! I thought. *This feels nice.*

Before this, my brain overanalyzed everything. I was always worrying about what people thought about me. I had been a reluctant altar boy at the Church of the Sacred Heart and hated it because everyone could see me up at the front. If I'd had a choice, I'd have been keeping a low profile at the back somewhere. At certain times during the service I had to ring the bell, but I always fucked it up because I was thinking about it too much. I was either too early or too late. Same shit with the water and wine. You're supposed to go pour it in the priest's chalice at a specific moment, but I was always messing that up too. It was mortifying.

I was on a Gaelic football team for years, but every time the ball got passed to me I couldn't make my mind up where to go or what to do. Before I could make a move, I'd get nailed by a player from the other team. Every year I got awarded the most free kicks. A good tactic for our team was to pass the ball to me in a dangerous position as I was sure to get nailed and receive a free for our side. But that just made me more anxious.

My childhood wasn't any more fucked up than most. My parents hit me, but only when I did something wrong. Everyone in Ireland hit their kids back then. There was only one kid I knew of whose dad didn't hit him. Instead, his dad made him write fifty lines about whatever he'd done wrong. We all thought that was daft and told him his dad was a pussy.

For whatever reason, I *always* felt stressed, but after swigging down some deep draughts of warm beer on that bus, I felt relaxed. After a few more, I even felt confident. Suddenly, I didn't care what anybody thought of me. Everything was right with the world. *Fuck. This is what it's all about. This is why all these people are drinking.* This was just what I had been missing. And just what I needed!

In my English class around this time, I remember our teacher, Mad Jack, asking "Why do people drink?" We all shrugged our shoulders. It just seemed to be the thing to do in Ireland. "The reason that people drink," he said, "is to get out of their heads." Yes! It now made perfect sense to me in this moment. The can of beer I was drinking on the way home from Galway that day was doing just that. It took me out of my head. Although I am pretty sure Mad Jack had other intentions, all I could think was, *Sound as a pound! Mad Jack was right!*

After that, I decided that drinking was going to be a thing for me. It gave me a feeling of ease and comfort that I could not manufacture on my own.

I don't know when comfort and ease stopped being my reason for drinking. At some point I crossed that invisible line, where drinking became something I *had* to do, instead of something I *wanted* to do. I'm not sure if I ever could control it, even from the beginning. But the consequences and situations became wilder and wilder, and there was no way to stop it. Drinking had become something much darker.

Until I found myself on August 31, 2010, sitting in my truck on the side of Fulton Street in San Francisco, a .22-caliber pistol in my hand, ready to blow my brains out.

In retrospect, a .22 was a lousy choice for the task at hand. The bullets are too small. Putting one through my skull might have only resulted in permanent brain damage. That was far from the desired outcome. Unless I had hollow points, which expand on impact and would have made swiss cheese out of my brain. I can't remember which were in the gun that day.

Like so many Irish before me, I had come to America hoping to make my way in the Land of Opportunity. For me, that meant the opportunity to get better cocaine. By that measure, I was an incredible immigrant success story. So successful, in fact, that I was ready to kill myself right there on the famous streets of San Francisco.

An addict who's committed to seeking help requires one of two things: the inner strength to recognize they have a problem, followed by the decision to do something about it; or hitting rock bottom. Or, as they say in twelve-step programs, "Admit you're powerless over drugs and alcohol and your life is unmanageable." For me, it was the latter. I had passed those warning signposts on the road to destruction countless times over the years and had missed or ignored them. First, I needed to hit rock bottom, but the problem is that when you are in it, you don't know what the bottom is.

The irony was that I always assumed I was the first type—a tough guy, honest with himself, who could quit anytime it felt like things were getting out of hand. Or I often had this idea in my head that I would quit at some time in the future, maybe when I was thirty, or forty. In fact, I had decided to quit several times. For an alcoholic or drug addict, this usually happens when the heat is on. When my girlfriend got pregnant with my first child, I realized it was time to be responsible and quit partying. But then that sneaky little bastard voice in my head made a persuasive point: There was no need to stop partying just because my girlfriend was pregnant—the time to stop partying was when the kid was born. I had more time.

Of course, when the kid was born, it seemed ridiculous to stop drinking and doing drugs for the benefit of a little baby who didn't know when he was pissing or shitting himself. (Both of which I actually did on occasion while drunk, so who am I to point fingers? Accidents happen.) I decided to keep on doing what I was doing until the kid was old enough for it to have an effect on him.

Moving the goal line like this is a method a lot of addicts employ, and I was masterful at it. It allowed me to keep on abusing myself while telling myself it was a conscious decision, that "I could quit anytime." One time, I stayed dry for three months, so *clearly* I could stop altogether if I really wanted to. A real alcoholic couldn't stop for three months, could he? I had heard alcoholics drank in the morning, so I made sure never to drink before noon. I had heard alcoholics drank at home, so I always drank at a bar. Alcoholics get DUIs, so I made sure I never got one, because I always used cocaine before getting in my truck (or driving anywhere) to balance things out.

These lines of reasoning meant the only option for me was hitting rock bottom.

The beginning of the end began in 2009. I was in San Francisco, building houses by day and selling cocaine and Viagra by night.

I built houses because after months of working for a moving company, I realized I'd never make real money that way. A buddy of mine worked construction and got me my first job as a carpenter.

I sold cocaine because it was my favorite drug. The more you take, the more you need, so it made sense to buy in bulk. And if you're buying in bulk, you might as well sell some to other people. Having good cocaine makes you popular in party circles. Cocaine felt like it was fixing my adult insecurities the way that alcohol solved my adolescent anxieties. Giving people the stuff that could make them happy was my purpose. I had taken to this role like a duck to water. At the time, I didn't know what my purpose would be if I wasn't playing this role. Between the two, I felt like I was totally in control while also out of my own head, as Mad Jack had said.

Sound as a pound!

I sold Viagra because coke makes you horny, but too much coke makes you limp. There's a fine line between doing the right amount of coke to fuck all night, and too much, which results in "coke dick" and a very disappointed woman. I could usually walk this particular tightrope, but some of my customers couldn't. Providing them with the little blue pills took the guessing out of the game.

At the time, I was in a gang. I've been in a lot of gangs down through the years, but in this particular gang I was the only Irishman. Actually, I was the only white dude. They were an Asian gang, and I ended up with them for the simple reason that they had the best cocaine, which makes complete sense to an addict.

I am pretty sure these Asians had the best cocaine in America! It was Peruvian, the shiny, flaky, glossy-rock type, not the dull, dusty, recompressed powdery shite that was mixed with that stuff for numbing teething babies' gums. Fish scale Charlie (or Barley as we Irish in America call it) at its finest. These Asian fellas were also highly reliable and utterly professional, a rarity in gangs. I was the loose cannon. By far. As well as the tallest. The other members didn't even do coke. They accepted me because I was trust-worthy and always paid in cash. I think they also found me entertaining.

Things were going great with my legal work (construction) and my illegal work (dealing drugs), but at home things were falling apart. My wife had a fairly quiet temperament, but we fought constantly, mostly due to the fact that I wasn't around much...and the drugs. She knew what she was getting into when we married, as much as anybody can know what it will be like to have an addict as a partner. There was just no way in the moment that I said "I do" that I would become a solid citizen who spent his off-time driving a minivan to Ikea.

I tried to do better. I made promises to be around more, even though I had no idea where to find the time. Then I realized that if I could make a big score, I could stop working so much...construction, at least.

A day or two later the idea came to me. My buddies Joey and Amos approached me with a great tip. There was a safe in a business office in Haight-Ashbury crammed with gold bars! Why? Who knows? Joey and Amos were tweekers who were not big on details or follow-through. All we needed was a way to blow the safe, and I immediately knew how...

Thermite—a mixture of iron oxide and aluminum that can burn through steel. (Place it on the engine block of a real car like a 1977 Mustang, ignite it with a blowtorch, and it will tear through the whole thing. I know this because of some trouble I got into back in Ireland.) I got everything together, made the thermite, and "borrowed" a blowtorch from a work site. It was on!

That's when Joey and Amos got pinched. I was having my doubts about the veracity of the story anyhow, and was ready to put them and the job behind me, except my wife found the thermite in my closet and thought the brownish powder was cocaine. I'm glad she didn't snort it to check. She just threw it in the garbage. I tried explaining that it was not drugs, that it was something I was doing for *us*, but it all fell on deaf ears.

The friction between us hit a new high and then I got some news that really shook me up. My girlfriend had been raped by someone she was see-ing on the side.

I took that news badly, and things began unraveling quickly. It all boiled down to "drunk logic" or "drug logic." The problem was not that my marriage was damaged to the point that I had a girlfriend. The problem was that her honor had been violated! PLUS, he must have known she was with me! At the least, my girlfriend telling me meant I needed to take action or risk looking like a pussy. If you're a criminal and someone hurts somebody close to you, the only course of action is to be the judge, jury, and executioner. In my confused state, there was only one path of action: Kill the fucker!

I went about planning the hit. But it is not as easy to kill someone as people think, even for a criminal such as myself. First, I had to find the guy. One of my customers was a private detective called Jon. He loved his cocaine, and he loved to be peed on by hookers, but he was good at finding people. I explained the situation to him, and he located the guy. Now, I had the guy's picture and an address. I just needed someone to kill him. If I did it, I'd be the first person the cops would question after his body was found, so I had to find a hitman.

The first person I thought of was Norteno Joe, an HVAC man who was, as his name would imply, also a Norteno, part of the northern Mexican mafia. He had just served five years in San Quentin and was out on parole. We worked together on the same jobsite. I bought coke off him and his brother sometimes. The interesting thing about gangsters is that they are more likely to be working on a construction site or in an accountant's office than roaming the streets doing nefarious deeds. It isn't a job. In most cases, it is just what people do to make ends meet. In that way, your average gangster is far more normal than you might think, and more likely to live closer to you than you might like.

Joe and I were buddies, so I rang him up. I said, "Can you talk on this line?" He said he could, so I explained the situation and told him I needed this fucker killed. "Can you do it?" I asked. He said he could—for five thousand dollars. "Fuck Joe, that's a lot of money. I'll give you two thousand." He wouldn't do it for two. I had to keep looking.

I went to Ronald, my point man in the Asian gang. He was an investment banker, but also an organized crime figure who supplied me with cocaine. I explained the situation and asked if they would do it, but he said they would only kill someone who had fucked the gang over. They couldn't take a contract for personal reasons.

Some people would have quit at this point. The thing about drug addicts is that we are tenacious, and I knew I had to get vengeance and kill this guy—for some reason that was getting foggier and foggier. I only knew that I had to do it! It seemed that Joe was my only option. I just needed five thousand dollars. There had to be some place I could get it. I didn't have the thermite anymore, and I didn't think the safe stuffed with gold bars was anything more than Joey and Amos's meth-fueled dream. How could I get the money?! I needed a drink to sort this out, and that gave me an idea.

It's not around anymore, but back in the day there was this IRA (FYI—the Irish terrorist group, not an American pension account.) bar in San Francisco that laundered money for them. You could go there on a Friday evening and there would be a half a million behind the bar.

Lots of Irish Americans romanticize the IRA (Irish Republican Army), often thinking of them as brave freedom fighters attacking the evil British rather than a terrorist group with guns and bombs. As a result, there are a lot of successful Irish-American businesses that shelter them or help them out in any way they can for "the cause."

If you were an illegal contractor or had a problem with the IRS or something, you could go into that bar with your check, and they'd give you your desired amount in cash, minus a nice tip for the barman. That laundered the money for the terrorists.

I thought about this bar and said, "Fuck it. Why don't I just rob it?" It was so simple. Cocaine gave me great ideas like this all the time, along with the balls to follow through on them. I just had to knock over a bar that was a front for a violent terrorist group. Then I would have the money to pay Joe and a lot left over. I was a drunk, coked-up genius!

The problem was that it was a two-man operation. One person would need to watch the customers while the other went back to get the money from the safe. I asked a couple of guys I knew, but all of them were too scared to join me. Or, as I thought, too stupid to see the elegant brilliance of my plan. I thought maybe I could do it with my girlfriend, but she was not into it at all. Even though I was doing this for her! Sort of. (Drunk logic: The problem is not the copious amount of drugs that I take or that I have a failing marriage and a girlfriend. The problem isn't even that I have to kill somebody who did a bad thing. The problem is that I don't have the money to do it. And my girlfriend won't help.)

I'll admit I romanticized things a bit, thought it could be a Bonnie and Clyde sort of thing, so I persisted. There was no convincing her, though. It's hard to make an armed robber out of an accountant. Since I was drunk and high, I was incensed at her lack of understanding and vision.

When my big score, the solution to all my problems, fell apart, so did I.

A quick inventory of my life said it all. I had been planning a hit, an armed robbery, and I was doing so much cocaine that my nose felt like it was going to fall off. My marriage was in shit and so was my relationship with my girlfriend. I had also failed at all my most recent attempts in criminality.

Like any good addict, though, I soldiered on, doing tons of cocaine and drinking copiously. But it was joyless. I felt like shit and was spiraling into a deep depression. I remember crossing the street sometimes wishing that a bus would just fucking hit me and put me out of my misery. My life felt unnervingly narrow. Suicidal thoughts became more frequent and more vivid, to the point where I knew I needed a break from all the cocaine and alcohol.

I thought, maybe if I quit drinking *and* doing drugs I could solve the other problems in my life and stop imagining ways to off myself. If it was possible, I never wanted to drink or get high again. Even though I had said this and meant it many times before, as soon as I'd crawled out of the hole I'd sunk into with all my dark thoughts, my mind always seemed to revert to the notion that I was fine as is, that things were better than I'd thought, and I was free to return to doing what I loved.

I hoped this time was different. I felt I'd gotten as good a look at the bottom as I wanted to see. For the next couple of weeks, I went to work every day. I didn't drink or get high. I was determined. My coke was gone and I had no intention of buying more, because it would be impossible to sell without doing some myself.

Prior to all this, I had worked with an Irish guy called Bernard. He was a bit younger, but a proper mountain man from Galway. He looked like a hunk from the cover of one of those Harlequin romance novels, big and strong with a full beard before hipsters made them fashionable. A good, decent guy, he was one of the publicly sober Irishmen in San Francisco. I knew that he'd had a problem with coke and drinking, that he'd started going to meetings and turned his life around. Things seemed to be going well for him. While working together on a holiday home in Tahoe, he gave me his number. "If ya ever want to get sober, give me a call." That's all he said. I peppered him with questions about sobriety, how it worked, how he'd pulled it off. I was curious, but he didn't give much away. In some ways, I made fun of him, asking sarcastic questions like whether he meditated. He took it in stride, smiled, and said, "Yeah. I walk around with a little fuckin' Buddha in me pocket! Ya bollocks."

He never said I had a problem. He never said I needed to get sober. He knew I had a problem, but he didn't judge or preach. He only gave me his number and let me know he was there when I needed him.

Now, I remembered him giving me that number, but I still thought I could stay sober on my own. Maybe I would be strong enough to do this. After those first couple of weeks, however, it became painfully evident that I couldn't. Driving home from work, I could feel my body wanting to go to the bar. I didn't want to go there. I didn't want to drink, but I could feel something fucking pulling me to do it. Something that wasn't me wanted me to do it again. It was like being possessed. This had obviously been with me all along and I was just now becoming aware of it. This was why I could never take it or leave it. I started thinking about Bernard. But I didn't call him.

In the final week of August 2010, I ended up going on what would be my last run. I had no intention of stopping at the time. It wasn't planned, and I had no idea that would be the end.

It started when somebody put me in touch with an undertaker from Dublin. A young guy in his twenties, pretty much the same age as me, he was coming for Burning Man, that giant desert rave, and wanted some cocaine. Apparently, undertakers like their Barley as much as the next fella. (When we were doing the deal, I made some chitchat with him and asked what he did for a living. He said, "Eh, I do the funerals," in a thick Dublin accent. Think about that the next time you're at a funeral. The guy in charge of your loved ones' remains might be a little cokehead. He's driving the hearse but planning a rager in the desert next week.) This undertaker wanted a half ounce of coke, so I bought a full ounce and kept half for myself, which I ended up doing all by myself over a period of about five days.

I stopped caring and just started snorting coke and drinking bottles of vodka. Days and nights blurred into each other. I fell into despair and found myself at the end of my tether. I rummaged through my drawers like a thief looking for hidden loot. After turning my apartment inside out, I found what I was looking for: Bernard's number. Just as I was about to call him, I got a call from Joe.

He had been charged with a DUI and desperately needed money, so he was willing to do the hit for two thousand. We were on! This snapped me out of my panic. I quickly convinced myself that my recent decline had been unduly caused by this unresolved situation. This was the way to get everything back on track. There was just one problem: I had to get him a gun. Given the discount he was offering, he wasn't willing to absorb the expense and insisted that I cover the cost of procuring a firearm. I had a gun, but it was legally owned. (If you're gonna kill someone, even if someone else pulls the trigger, don't use your own gun. Say you have someone killed with a .38 and the police know you have one registered in your name. They just have to get the gun and do a ballistics check, and they know that that's the gun that was used. If you're going to kill somebody, you need to get a separate gun.)

I called my friend Silva and asked him to get me one. He said no problem, just meet him in the Mission District. I had been awake for three days, kind of sleepwalking around, doing lots of coke, and feeling really out of my head. This must have been pretty apparent to Silva. I don't remember a whole lot of the conversation, but when he saw me he didn't want to give me the gun, probably because he thought I would get caught. One way or the other, I left empty-handed because he didn't feel comfortable giving me a gun in that condition.

I started driving back to my place in the Richmond District. While heading up Fulton, I noticed a cop car behind me. The blow I still had left wasn't much, but it was in my glove compartment and was enough to put me away for a good while. After twenty blocks, it became clear the cop car was following me. I started sweating, trying not to look in the mirror. Eventually their lights came on. Then the siren. *Fuck.* I was done. Then, suddenly, they turned and sped off in the opposite direction. I nearly had a heart attack. My heart was beating through my chest. I pulled over and smoked five cigarettes, one after the other. I couldn't take it anymore. Things weren't working. They never had. And it seemed like they never would, either. Total despair and hopelessness. There was no point in continuing. There was no friendly direction anywhere. I was out of ideas.

Except for one—the real solution to all my problems. I reached for my gun, the legal .22 I kept in my truck, cocked it, and pressed it to my head. That didn't seem right. I put the barrel in my mouth and tried to summon the courage to pull the trigger. My breathing was heavy. I saw my red face in the mirror with my dilated pupils. It didn't look like me at all. Someone else was looking back at me.

I was so tired.

The idea came to me that maybe things would get better if I could stop doing drugs and drinking. Maybe.

I called Bernard, who seemed surprised.

"Richie! How are ya?" he exclaimed.

I put the gun on my lap and murmured, "Bernard, I think I have a problem with the drink and the drugs. Will ya take me to a meeting?"

He got serious immediately. "I'll pick ya up outside your house."

I gave him my address and thanked him. That was that. Just making that call gave me a sense of relief, the first honest slice of peace I had felt in years.

That night I slept like a log.

STEP TWO

NOW I HAVE TO BELIEVE IN GOD?! AHH, FOR FUCK'S SAKE...

---♦---

A HIGHER POWER CAN RESTORE ME TO SANITY?

---♦---

"RICHARD STEPHENS, WE ARE CHARGING you with Offenses Against The State Act."

Fuck. These were the type of charges given to the IRA and other paramilitary groups accused of terrorism. "That's crazy," I said, trying to play it cool while feeling pretty sure the cops could tell I was pissing myself. "I didn't do anything."

"Oh, yeah? Well, your partner in crime just gave you up. Told us everything." They tossed a stack of fake IDs onto the table. "Forging State Documents. That's a crime against the state, Richie."

I was sixteen, facing serious prison time, and wondering, *How the hell did I get here?*

Just a few years earlier, I was an altar boy, scared of my own shadow. Now I was well on my way to being a gangster.

I guess it all started when I was fifteen, with a little innocent knacker drinking. Knacker drinking is drinking outside in a secluded area, like a parking lot or field, where no one will catch you. It's what you did in Ireland before you were old enough to get into bars and nightclubs. If you couldn't steal booze from home, you either went to a liquor store that didn't check IDs, or you sent in someone older to buy it for you. Once you had your booze, you headed for your knacker drinking location and got to it.

I believe it's called "knacker drinking" because it was associated with Irish Travellers. "Knacker" is a derogatory term for Irish gypsies, or "Travellers" as they like to be called nowadays. If you called a Traveller a "knacker" to their face, they would probably kick seven different colors

31

of shit out of you. Travellers always had problems with bars and hotels because people didn't want to serve them. Right or wrong, they had a reputation for fighting, and proprietors didn't want to risk trouble by letting them in. As a result, they became known for drinking outside.

I grew up in a small town called Cavan. It didn't even have a traffic light until I was a teenager, and then all the rednecks had to learn how to use it. (Before you ask, yes, we have rednecks in Ireland, too. They also like country music and have non-progressive ways of thinking.) Occasionally you'd see a tractor run the light because these guys hadn't quite figured out that "red means stop and green means go!" Bejaysus. The wonders of science.

Technically I lived outside of Cavan Town in the middle of nowhere. Arva was my nearest town, and it only had around four hundred people, a couple of grocery stores, and a church. There wasn't really a whole lot to do that I could see except drink. Arva had fourteen pubs back then. Party central! Cavan is also always cold and wet. Unless you wanted to die of hypothermia, you had to get whatever booze you could, head to your favorite knacker drinking location, drink the shit out of it, then get the hell back inside.

A quick rundown on what we drank as kids:

- ✔ **Buckfast Tonic Wine:** a tonic wine from England. "Made by the Benedictine monks of Buckfast Abbey," said the brown bottle. Different drinks can make you different kinds of drunk. Guinness drunk feels different from vodka drunk. Buckfast drunk was a special kind of drunk, a crazy kind of drunk, like speed or something. You could break things or climb things on Buckfast. A knacker drinking favorite.

- ✔ **Dutch Gold:** a cheap beer that came in large cans. You could buy four of them for five pounds. Dutch Gold gave me the Dutch courage that most drinking gave me. Another favorite.

- ✔ **Poteen:** Irish moonshine for when you couldn't get the other stuff. Even though it was illegal, everyone knew who was making it. And it was in every family's liquor cabinet.

Whatever I drank, I made sure to drink way too much of it. As I said, my first drink got me out of my head. After that, there was no point in stopping. Drinking kept me from thinking about what was really troubling me. But that troubled feeling only left me while I drank. Later, it was always lurking there. I probably couldn't have told you what it was then, but I can now.

It was fear.

It's not like I had a bad childhood. My parents were honest, decent, working-class people who got along well with our neighbors and the community. The only thing different about them was that my dad was Protestant and my mother was Catholic. But that difference felt huge to a young lad who only wanted to fit in.

Ireland is a beautiful and strange country, but one with a split personality. Northern Ireland is mainly Protestant and Unionist; the south is mainly Catholic and Republican. Cavan is right near the border of Northern Ireland, and has a strong split personality of its own. Even though 90 percent of the people are Catholic, it still has a much larger percentage of Protestants than nearby counties. My house had Catholic and Protestant living under one roof. This was exceptionally uncommon when my parents married in 1980 at the height of "The Troubles." You could compare a Protestant marrying a Catholic to a white person marrying a black person in the fifties in America.

In the days of The Troubles, if you were a Catholic and wanted to marry a Protestant, you needed special dispensation from the Pope! You went to your local priest, and he asked the bishop, and it went all the way up the line to the big guy in the Vatican. I guess John Paul II was cool with it because my folks got married in a Catholic church. There was just one condition—us kids had to be raised Catholic. This wasn't a problem for my dad. Even though he was Protestant, he wasn't very observant. I don't remember him ever going to Protestant services, except weddings and funerals. For my mom, it was the most important thing in the world. She was a strict Catholic—a Catho-holic as I used to say—so I was raised in the Catholic Church.

And I *felt* Catholic. As nervous as I was to be an altar boy, I still took pride in my religion. But I quickly learned how tough it could be to have one Catholic parent and one Protestant. I barely knew any other "mixed" kids. Pretty much everyone was either all Catholic or all Protestant. The Catholics knew my father was a Protestant and always looked on me with suspicion, as if I was a spy in their camp—to do what, I had no idea, but I never felt completely accepted. To the Protestants, I was just a turncoat, someone who had abandoned them to consort with the other side. I never felt like I truly belonged anywhere. And that's where my fear came from.

Twelve-step programs talk of needing to find a higher power in your life, one that isn't alcohol or drugs. Catholic school could have been the perfect place to find my higher power, a place that might have quieted the fear inside of me. Instead, the school I was sent to was a living hell. Everyone there seemed to feel it was their God-given mission to put as much fear into me as possible.

I naively thought starting secondary school would be a fresh start, with new kids who didn't know my father was Protestant. But there was no hiding it. In Ireland, all the Catholics have Irish-sounding names like Brady or O'Reilly. Stephens is clearly a Protestant name. They preached at school about loving your neighbor, but I guess not if he was a fucking Protestant. The type of rudimentary history they taught was pure fighting talk for armchair Republicans, simple victim and oppressor shit. "Grrrr, the English took our land!" stuff that made people's blood boil.

Fuel for The Cause.

There was a lot of hypocrisy like that on display. I had a bunch of teachers who were priests. They were supposed to be men of God—but if they were men of God, then most of them were his B team, at best. They would hit you, or get angry and pick their nose in front of you, just to show how little respect they had for you, how little your opinion of them mattered. I don't think any of these dicks were diddling kids, but it's not like I would have been shocked if I heard they were.

The students were just as bad. Sectarian young pricks in my school talked shit about Protestants and called them "blacks" or "black cunts." This came from the term "the Black and Tans"—not the whiskey, but the brutal British army unit from the First World War who came to Ireland and massacred innocent people as a result of the guerilla war with the IRA.

A popular form of bullying in my school was "jocking." Americans know it as an "atomic wedgie." Basically, someone would come up behind you and yank the waistband of your underwear all the way up over your head, ripping them off you. Many a testicle was knocked up into the stomach from this procedure. A kid with the last name Stephens was a prime target. Fortunately, I was a fast runner and never got chafed, but I walked the halls of that place always looking over my shoulder. For a shy, awkward, mixed-religion kid, it wasn't the best atmosphere.

Instead of finding a higher power, I just found a higher level of fear.

But then, when I was sixteen, everything changed because of my love of curry chips.

In Ireland, after a big night out, everyone ended up at the "chippers" (fast food restaurants) to finish things off with a big plate of greasy food. For me, nothing tasted better after some knacker drinking than curry chips, so I'd head over, get my food, and settle in for a night of entertainment.

If you want a recipe for violent chaos, all you have to do is take all the drunken Irishmen who haven't gotten laid at the clubs and pour them into a small, crowded restaurant. Just sit back and enjoy the show. Drunken, aggressive Irishmen tend to fight with each other, and Cavan had lots of them! A foot stepped on here, the wrong look at someone there, and fists would start flying.

I loved watching every moment of it. I was still a shy kid, but it was very exciting to watch this violence. The suspense leading up to each row was almost as good as watching the melee itself. *Is this redneck gonna allow this townie wanker to keep winking at his woman?...Fuck me, someone just threw a tub of brown sauce at that big bollocks at the counter....* It was like watching an action movie. Bodies would go flying and land on top of tables where other customers were eating. It was great. And no one seemed to be having more fun than the fellas beating the shit out of each other!

I remember walking home on those nights, still high off the energy from those ne'er-do-wells throwing each other all over the place. There was something to these guys...there was strength...and freedom...but there was something else—they were *fearless*. I wanted to be like that! Every time I left my house, I worried about being caught drinking, or getting beat up, or just doing something embarrassing. I would look at these guys and think, *How the fuck are they not afraid of anything? How can I be like that???*

The answer came to me through Walter, who was a year older than me and the perfect "starter bad boy" for a kid like me looking to inch a little closer to the fire. My mom didn't like or approve of Walter because his father used to be a terrorist. Walter told me his dad was an IRA man in Northern Ireland during The Troubles of the 1970s and '80s and had to flee Belfast after blowing up a paratrooper in an army barracks. The type of bomb he used attached to the inside handle of a door. When the handle turns, it spills mercury on the detonator and blows the door up—along with the person who opened it. People use the tubes of pens to hold the mercury, but Walter's dad had been sloppy—he'd used a tube from his work location, the Royal Post Office. This was written on the side, so the Royal Ulster Constabulary knew it was someone who worked at the post office. The net was closing in, so he bounced south of the border and started a new life in Cavan.

One of the perks of hanging around with Walter was that his parents didn't give a shit what we did. I could stay over at his house and we could get as drunk as we wanted and his parents wouldn't give a fuck. He had a way longer leash than I did. At my house, I had to either hide my drinks or steal from the liquor cabinet. At Walter's house, we could keep our shit in the fridge. At my house, my poor mother would be waiting in the kitchen at 4 a.m. when I strolled in drunk. At Walter's house, they didn't give a shit if we were gone for a week!

I was breaking rules and having fun. Still, I felt like we were kids playing in the sandbox while the grown-ups were having the *real* fun at the bars and clubs. This was where the real action was, where the troublemakers spent most of their night with adult women, and I was dying to be a part of it. But there was one big problem: The drinking age was eighteen and I didn't have a fake ID. I sure as hell wasn't going to let that stop me! First, I tried climbing in through the bathroom windows. It worked a few times, but the bouncers kept catching me. Fuck it, I really needed to get an ID.

An ID card was basically a blue card with your name, date of birth, photo on the front, and a Garda or police stamp—with a date and signature on the back. I was determined to make a couple for Walter and myself. My computer had Microsoft Windows 95 so I got on the Microsoft Paint application, measured up the ID, and inputted that as my canvas size. Copying the fonts required a lot of trial and error before I finally settled on Courier. When the ID came out of the printer, it was too perfect. I figured that if you smudged it with your finger while the ink was wet, it came out just like a real typewriter! The front was flawless.

Now came the tough part. How would I get the Garda stamp? After figuring out the smudge on the front of the card, I knew I could make a pink square and then smudge it to look like a wet stamp. It didn't work. Again, it looked too perfect. I tried printing it onto glossy photograph paper so I could smudge it better. It was impressive, but backwards! Eventually, I inverted it and printed it onto an old photo. Then, while the ink was still wet, stamped the photo on the card, and *boom*—a damn near exact copy of the Garda ID.

Once our IDs were done, they needed to be laminated, but I couldn't bring them into a store to do this. Stores tend to alert the cops when you try to make them an accessory to forging government documents. But you can buy lamination slips, so I brought some home and was able to DIY them using a hot iron and a towel over the ID and laminate.

Now came the moment of truth. Nervous as hell, Walter and I walked up to one of the Cavan nightclubs. When the bouncer asked for our IDs, we handed them over. He gave them a quick look, handed them back, and nodded us inside.

I wasn't thinking about any higher power at the time, but this was definitely the holy land! We would hit the bars and nightclubs whenever we could. I loved feeling like an adult. I would show up, the bartenders would know my regular drink, I'd get shit-faced and have no trouble talking to women—older women who would sleep with me. High school girls were too uptight to have sex, but that wasn't a problem for these women. I was living the dream, drinking elbow to elbow with the real bad boys, and even getting into the occasional scrap at the chippers myself.

But drinking in nightclubs was expensive. My job as a gas station attendant paid minimum wage, so I wasn't earning enough to satisfy the needs of a young alcoholic in the making. Walter didn't have much money either. We could finally get into the clubs, but we couldn't afford to drink at them.

Walter had started telling people at school what a genius I was at making IDs. He asked if I could make more so he could sell them, said we'd be business partners. I'd make lots of money, enough to drink and go out as much as I wanted. That's all I needed to hear.

We started off small, making four or five IDs, but the situation quickly escalated to the point where I was making fucking tons of IDs for people all over the school. I was even making them for kids at other schools who I had never met before. Then something amazing happened. I became popular.

Suddenly, the jocks who'd pushed me around and treated me like shit were kissing my ass because I could make IDs for them. I was the key to their freedom. Nobody cared if I was Protestant now! I went from being a bit of a nerdy loser weakling to somebody cool—one of the bad boys.

Being bad was exhilarating. People looked at me and treated me differently. I no longer felt like an outsider, a scared kid who didn't belong anywhere. Now, whether I was drinking at the bars or walking the halls, I felt accepted, admired, and maybe even a little feared for my crazy streak. Drinking and misbehaving was the perfect solution to my problem. I wasn't afraid anymore.

A pattern for my life of crime started here. In this case, I made a fake ID, liked what it got me but couldn't afford it, so I started selling fake IDs. When I first tried drugs, I liked them but couldn't afford to buy as much as I wanted, so I started dealing them. Like anything good, you want more of it. The cycle just feeds itself.

At the time, making money off the IDs, drinking in the clubs, getting laid, feeling fearless, life was perfect. Then Walter got pinched by the cops and ratted on me. I found myself facing a long prison sentence for crimes against the state.

When the cops first came after me, I couldn't believe it. One of the reasons I agreed to sell fake IDs with Walter was because he'd asked me to, and I thought I could trust him. I figured that because his dad was a terrorist, he or anyone from his family would never rat. If Walter got caught, he'd keep his mouth shut, tight as a drum. But sitting in that interrogation room, looking at all the evidence lying on the table in front of me, it was clear Walter had flipped. The cops told me Walter's old man had ratted on me as well. What the fuck? What about the IRA code of silence? Turns out that having built a new life in the "Free State," Walter's old man didn't want anything to do with the fake ID operation of his youngest son and his younger dickhead friend.

I had planned on denying everything, but it was clear that wasn't going to work, so I repented. "I'm sorry, officers. I won't do it again! I only made a few for my friends! I didn't realize it was this serious! I won't do it again." I figured since I wasn't eighteen I had a chance to avoid prison, but the cops weren't having it.

"There's one thing that still doesn't add up, Richie. Where did you get the Garda stamp?" They thought I had stolen one or maybe I was given one by somebody inside the station. The cops were worried they had a mole in a government office, or I had a cache of pirated Garda stamps somewhere. That's why they were pushing the Offenses Against The State Act charge. They thought I was a bloody terrorist!

So, I explained to them how I had made them, using a backwards print onto a glossy photo and then using it like a stamp while it was still wet. They let that sink in and eventually replied, "Jaysas ha?!?" Even though they couldn't completely grasp my explanation, they were impressed. I might have been an expert sixteen-year-old forger, but they were actually relieved they didn't have to investigate another cop in their station or a robbery right there under their noses. They were just dealing with some sort of entrepreneurial computer "genius" who knew how to manufacture the Garda stamp. (That's what made you a genius in Cavan back then.)

While I was sitting there in the interrogation room, knowing I could be looking at some serious prison time, I did what a lot of people do. I prayed to God to get me out of that mess. "Please God, if you get me out of this, I'll never do anything like this again. Please please, God, help me."

Then the cops let me go, with just a warning to never do it again. My prayers had been answered.

Soon after, like most people, I forgot about that offer I'd made to God to do the right thing. I don't know if I forgot about it or if I didn't believe God had gotten me out of it, but one way or the other, I didn't change. I kept drinking and getting into trouble. And I really felt good about myself and my life.

I had found my higher power after all—drink, and then drugs—and I worshipped them faithfully. They ran my life. Until they ran it into the ground, which is what brought to me the doors of the Irish Center in San Francisco, waiting for my first meeting to begin. Standing there, completely sober, I felt that old enemy sneaking back—fear.

Before I started drinking and misbehaving, I wanted to be invisible. One of my biggest fears was speaking in front of other people. I knew enough about twelve-step meetings to know that that was exactly what I was expected to do, and it scared the shit out of me, especially telling them the truth about all the drinking and getting high. It was embarrassing. In the past, it had crossed my mind to go to a meeting, sit in the back of the room, give a fake name, learn what I could, and then get the fuck out of there, but that was off the table now. Bernard knew who I was, so I couldn't pull that shit.

Outside the Irish Center, there were a few guys hanging out. I didn't want to hang around there in case anyone might see me going in, like it was a porno store or something. But the Irish dudes out front seemed really nice. One of them, Steven, came up and asked if I was new. I told him I was. He asked if I thought I had a problem with drinking and drugs. I told him

I did. He asked why I thought that. I told him I had just tried to kill myself. He said, "Yeah, that'll do it."

I was in the right place.

I asked him how this shit worked, and in a strong Belfast accent, he said, "If your ass falls off, you don't take a drink. We don't take a drink no matter what."

We went inside to the meeting, and I sat down in the back. It was all men, mostly Irish guys I had never met before. This American dude called Dave shook hands with me and asked if I was new. I told him I was. He asked if I had a sponsor. I told him I didn't. He gave me his number and said if I wanted one I could give him a call.

At the start of the meeting, they asked if there were any new members. Everyone looked in my direction. They all knew somehow. I put my hand up and said, "My name's Richie. I'm an alcoholic and drug addict." I couldn't believe I actually said it. The words came out of my mouth without being prompted or anything. I figured I might as well be honest and give it a try, seeing as Bernard had taken the time to bring me. As soon as I said it, the whole room clapped! I was thinking, *Do you people know who I am? What I've done?* I'm sure some of them did know who I was, but they didn't care one way or the other. They were just happy to have a new man in there, who admitted he had a problem and was someone they could help. I couldn't believe that they actually applauded me and wanted to help with no strings attached.

I felt like I was the worst person in the room. And I probably was. To this day, I often am the worst person in the meeting for the stuff I've done during those crazy years. But these people didn't give a shit about that. All they cared about is that you came for help and that you were not misbehaving anymore. They were willing to help. Free of charge. It was weird.

My head was still foggy at this point. But a couple of things I can remember from that meeting hit me in the fucking heart. This one American dude put up his hand and started sharing some stories with the group. He said he was "restless, irritable, and discontented." When I heard those three words, I thought, *Fuck me pink. Restless, irritable, and discontented?!?* That's how I feel when I'm not drinking. I thought that it was only me who had these feelings. I didn't know what an alcoholic was really, and it struck me that apparently all alcoholics felt this way. The revelation was *Holy shit, there's more of them that feel the same way as I do. I'm not unique.* I had just thought an alcoholic was someone who couldn't handle their shit. I knew nothing about the mental traits of an addict, and I believed that the depressive feelings were unique to me for all those years, like maybe I was a psychopath, sociopath, or manic-depressive or something.

Another thing I remember hearing from that first meeting was a story one of the older Irish guys—Christy—told. He had gone to the dump to get rid of a load in his dump truck. He was just trying to reverse and dump the load when some dude started shouting at him. He saw some dickhead in his mirror screaming at him, "Hey, you can't dump that shit here!!!" Christy told us that he got so angry that he wanted to jump out of the truck and strangle him. He just wanted to choke the fucking life out of the guy. I could relate to this. I got these intense feelings of rage all the time, too, over nothing. Things would just set me off.

After hearing these two guys saying this kind of shit, I felt great relief. I had resigned myself years ago to the feeling that I would be fucked up forever, but now I had hope that maybe that wasn't my future. There seemed to be a solution. Here I was in a room full of people experiencing the exact same shit. I felt super positive about that meeting.

Until the very end.

On the wall was a big scroll with "the steps," all twelve of them. Some of the shit I read scared the hell out of me. One step was making amends to people I'd harmed. No fucking way was I going to make amends to people I had harmed. I had harmed a lot of people, and if I admitted to the stuff I had done, I could be sent to jail for the rest of my life.

Fuck. That. Shit.

It was the second step, though, that was starting to look like a bigger problem to me right then. "Come to believe that a higher power could restore you to sanity."

Fuck. I'd tried that. I was an atheist. The only thing that ever worked for me was booze and drugs. But to stay sober, an addict has to find something to replace them. Only what I now saw happening was definitely not going to work for me.

At the end of the meeting, everybody stood up out of their chairs and held hands. Couldn't believe that shit. No offense to Americans, but I could never imagine Irish men holding hands like that. But there we were! Even big, tough, hard Irish construction workers were holding hands.

Then they said the Lord's Prayer! That really freaked me out. *What the fuck is this shit?!* Immediately I thought that it must be a religious cult. I thought I had found an answer, thought I could see the beginning of a path out of the shitstorm I was in—and now this. This holding-hands bullshit and saying the "Our Father" really turned me off. I knew this had been too good to be true.

After years of bargaining, not believing, and generally laughing at people who believed in God, there I was, being asked to believe in a higher power. I knew right then my answer was going to be "no." It felt like a mistake. I thought, *I definitely won't be coming back here again, because I don't want to join no religion.*

Once I left the meeting, I waited outside for Bernard. Steven came up and said, "Well, you didn't get struck by lightning, did you?" Apparently not. I just wanted to get the fuck away from these weird religious freaks. As soon as possible.

Bernard took me to his truck. As soon as we got into the cab, he turned around, smiling. "Well, what did ya think?!"

I was still shaken from all the Jesus talk and said, "What the fuck was all that God shit?"

"What are ya talkin' about?"

I mentioned the hand-holding, saying the "Our Father," and the God stuff in the twelve steps.

"Never mind that shit!" he responded sharply.

"What?!"

"You don't have to believe in that shit," he said. "There's fuckin' Buddhists and Muslims and atheists and all kinds a people in these rooms. You don't have to believe in any of that shit. Just shut your mouth and come back to the meetings. Never mind that shit."

"Really?"

He said I didn't have to believe in anything I didn't want to believe in.

I thought about that for a moment. Fair enough. I sat back and felt myself relax. That was all I needed to hear.

I definitely didn't want to become a Catholic again. I just wanted to stop drinking and getting high. And these meetings, with these men who reminded me so much of myself and my problems, seemed like a real lifeline.

As Bernard drove me home, I had one nagging thought I couldn't shake:

> *I was giving up the only higher power that had ever worked for me, and I had nothing to replace it with. Would I need to believe in a higher power to stay sober?*

YOU CAN'T WORSHIP A DOORKNOB

---◈---

TURN YOUR WILL AND YOUR LIFE OVER TO A HIGHER POWER

---◈---

THEY SAY GOD CAN BRING you comfort in troubling times. So can booze and drugs. At least at the beginning, but eventually they turn on you and, over time, they give you more trouble than comfort. Then you end up in a worse position than where you started.

By the time I was sixteen, I was drinking regularly and running with the bad boys. Most nights, I drank so much that I got sick, and could barely move the next day. I'd also black out a fair amount. I'd go to a party and the next thing I knew I was waking up in a strange room—that's if I was lucky, because I woke up in some strange places outside too. It was all part of the deal though, because getting blackout drunk served its purpose—turning off my brain. Really feeling nothing. Pink Floyd knew what they were singing about with "Comfortably Numb."

Soon, though, the glamour and novelty of illegal drinking wore off, and things became a bit boring and mechanical, which gave all my old insecurities room to make their way back to the surface. Naturally, I tried drinking more, but that simple, clean oblivion was getting harder to find. The new problem was that I seemed unable to handle my drinking as well as everybody else. Some of the looks people gave me said, "That guy can't handle his shit." It was starting to become embarrassing.

It was time to move on to something else. I still liked my alcohol, but I needed a more powerful weapon in my arsenal. I needed drugs.

I had always been afraid to do drugs. I had heard about people OD'ing and seen what drugs could do to your brain. One of the more infamous guys I knew was "Divey." His real name was David, but in a Dublin accent the way they say Davie was "Divey." Divey was relatively normal until the age of eighteen, when he took some acid and had a bad trip. He had a nervous breakdown and developed schizophrenia. When Divey was in his early twenties, his brother "Kiddles" overdosed on heroin. Divey came home and found him on the kitchen floor with a needle in his arm. Kiddles survived, but Divey was so angry that he went to the dealer's house and lit it on fire—while the dealer and his girlfriend were asleep in bed. The couple made it out alive, but Divey was sent to jail for four years. That's when he began to take on a mythic quality, like the boogeyman. I remember meeting people my own age who told me that when they were kids they were scared that "Divey would come to get them."

I didn't want to end up like Divey, but at the time I was really into certain types of music, like The Doors. I read about them and knew they did a lot of drugs. I just couldn't stop wondering what it felt like to get high, and I convinced myself that marijuana might be okay to do. In Ireland at the time, though, there wasn't really any marijuana around, just cannabis resin or hash.

One drunken night, while I was out and about in Cavan Town, I bumped into Butler and McGrath, a couple of well-known druggies from "The Half Acre." The Half was the bad part of Cavan Town. Most of the shit-bags who got into trouble with the law lived there. Butler was short with blond hair, looked like a weasel, and acted like one. McGrath had dark hair and was tall, but he wasn't hated by everyone like Butler was. These guys had all kinds of fancy lingo I had never heard before, calling me "Sham" or "Soubla" or even "Soubleen," and started or finished every sentence with the word "hai." "Hai Sham, were you talkin' to dat Soubla before?!"

After some more small talk like this, they finally asked me a question I understood—did I want to buy any hash? I decided it was time to take the leap.

"How much is it?"

"I can give you a five spot," Butler said.

"Yeah," I said, "let's do it."

I didn't know what hash looked like or smelled like, but I knew it couldn't kill you, and I'd never heard of anyone developing schizophrenia after doing it. I handed over the money, and they gave me a little matchbox. Inside was a tiny, hard round ball, about a quarter inch in diameter. It had a kind of pungent smell, and I was convinced it wasn't cooking herbs or any of that shit. It was real hash! I asked them the best way to smoke it, and decent druggies that they were, they rolled a joint for me and we smoked it there and then. In Ireland, a joint was a mix of hash and tobacco, not straight weed like in America.

Before long, I was feeling just fine. I couldn't believe it had taken me so long to try this. Hash took me out of myself, but without the sickness and loss of motor skills that alcohol gave me. It was chill. Relaxed. This was a whole new world. This was what I obviously needed! I had no plans to quit drinking, but I knew I was going to make hash a regular part of my evenings out. I also knew enough to realize Butler and McGrath were unreliable fuckers, so I couldn't make a habit of buying off them. I needed to find someone else. In Cavan Town, the townies hung around the square by the post office. Boys wearing tracksuits and hair gelled straight down on their head—obvious crims. You could walk past them and they would say, "Do ya wanna buy some hash?" After that one smoke with Butler and McGrath, I now considered myself an expert, so I wouldn't get ripped off. I bought from these guys a few times, but every deal had me looking over my shoulder, wondering if I was about to get busted.

This was something new to worry about. I thought it was a healthy fear, though. This wasn't the previous gnawing kind from deep inside. It was actually exciting. It was smart to worry about getting arrested. And as long as I was smart, why not keep at this wonderful new thing that could take me out of my head in better and more beautiful ways?

When I started buying from my pal, Zippy, I felt even smarter. Zippy was a guy I knew from school, who was really friendly and not dangerous in the slightest—kind of like Slater from the movie *Dazed and Confused*. (He was called Zippy because he looked just like a puppet called Zippy from the children's TV show *Rainbow*. Picture a yellow Kermit, but not as cute.)

I didn't have to buy my drugs right out on the street, and I trusted Zippy. I had my first, very own drug dealer! It was so exciting!

Hash, and weed when I could get it, became my after-school snacks. I would smoke a lot at home, by myself—go up to my bedroom, roll a joint or use my newly purchased hash pipe, and smoke it out the window. I would lie down and listen to The Doors, Bob Marley, the sort of tunes that go well with hash. The music sounded different to me than it did before. It would really take me away. I never stopped to think that whatever it was taking me away from would be waiting once the high wore off.

When I graduated from high school, I also graduated to harder drugs. The National University of Ireland, Maynooth, was my fifth or sixth choice, but I got a C average in my exams so that's where I ended up. Maynooth is a small college town outside of Dublin, and I rented a house with a couple of straight shooters, but still did a lot of drinking and smoking hash. I was hanging around with some friends from home, Pat the Rat and Ferret. Pat was called "the rat" because he kinda looked like one (he wasn't a snitch), and Ferret was called that that because he talked really fast and sort of sounded like one. (Oddly enough, I knew two different guys called "Ferret." This was Cavan Ferret who I knew since I was twelve, not to be confused with Waterford Ferret, who was a new friend from college.) One night they introduced me to Tommo.

Tommo was from down south, a bit of a loner, but a good guy. He had long sideburns and walked with a swagger. He called everybody "Mush." Like a lot of first-year college students in Ireland, he was staying in "digs," which was basically renting a room from a family who would cook your food for you. People who were in digs don't usually have friends over, seeing as it's not really their house, so first-year students in digs tended to hang out in other students' houses. After Ferret brought Tommo around, he started hanging out with us.

Tommo was into ecstasy and was always trying to get me to take some. I was hesitant because of stories I'd read in the newspapers about how some kid tried ecstasy one time only and it killed him. Knowing my luck, I thought that would probably be me. One night, though, near the end of the school year, we were out drinking in the Leinster Arms, as usual. I had a good few pints in me.

"Mush, do ya wanna try one of these ecstasy?" Tommo says.

"No, I can't. That wouldn't be a good idea."

"You'll be grand," he reassured me. "They're not even strong, these ones."

"Really?"

"Yeah, try one, ta fuck."

I thought, *Alright, Tommo's smart, they don't seem to have killed him.* I trusted his word. He gave me a small beige cylindrical-shaped pill with the logo 007 on it. I took it into the bathroom and went into one of the stalls. I was definitely too scared to take it all, but I had never heard of anyone dying of half a pill, so I decided to be extra safe and took a quarter. When I came back out and he asked if I took it, I said, "Yeah," but I didn't tell him I'd only taken part of it in case he thought I was a pussy.

About a half hour later, he asked me if I was feeling it. I said I wasn't. He asked if I took it all, and I said I only took a half. "Mush, ya need to take a whole one. A half won't do nothing for ya. These are really light." *Fuck, okay.* I took the other quarter. Eventually I started to feel it. Coming up on ecstasy for the first time, my body and head were so full of euphoria, it was the best feeling I ever had in my life. The name "ecstasy" was the perfect way to describe it. I loved everybody. I was super happy. Dancing. The music sounded great. *Why isn't everybody in the world taking these all day every day?!*

Next came the other half of the pill. I ended up taking two pills that first night. It was like discovering alcohol all over again. I decided to do it all the time, thinking, *This is way better than drinking, way better than smoking weed.* Obviously, *this* was what was missing in my life.

Pretty soon I had Pat the Rat and Ferret taking them. At first, I was just handing out pills to anybody I liked, for the simple reason that ecstasy was so great! I was like a preacher spreading the good word, but instead I was telling everyone how ecstasy could help them enjoy their lives. The pills weren't cheap. They were like ten pounds each, and though I barely had any money, I couldn't stop giving them away. I felt like I was helping people.

Tommo saw what I was doing and said, "Mush, seeing as you're getting all these pills for all these other people as a favor, why don't ya get a bunch of them for yourself and ya can sell the rest of them and then ya get your own for free?" What? That had never occurred to me. It would certainly be the solution to my cash flow problem. But I also knew something else—that was dealing.

Being a bad boy was one thing; in Ireland, drinking and misbehaving usually fell into the "boys will be boys" category. But this was full-on crime, and I knew the penalties for being caught dealing were serious. This wouldn't be like the IDs where I was let off with a warning. I told Tommo this, and he said, "Mush, you're already dealing when ya get them for someone else. The charge is 'for sale or supply' so if you get them for someone else as a favor, the cops will do ya for dealing. You're already dealing them for free! Ya might as well make a few quid when you're already taking the risk."

Like so many other things on the crazy road I had chosen so far, this made perfect sense to me. I started dealing, and, without taking the time to really think about it, became a full-fledged criminal. Tommo taught me the ins and outs. Within a year, I was no longer just dealing, I was a wholesaler, sending hundreds of pills to different parts of Ireland with different people. I was always very careful about who I let deal for me. I was particularly careful about finding someone in Cavan, because I knew it was full of rats and you couldn't trust a lot of the criminals up there. That's where Ollie came in. He was an enterprising little fucker who came across as being smart and fairly put together. And his dad was a Sinn Féin councillor, so, just as I had with Walter and the counterfeit IDs, I thought a guy from a terrorist family would never snitch if he was caught. I mean, Walter was obviously the exception to the rule. Right? Ollie had a tattoo on his arm of a leprechaun with his fists raised. I asked him what it was. "Fightin' Irish bai!" Ollie had no idea that this tattoo was an American football college team. He just thought it was tough and cool. I had no idea myself until I came to the US. A bunch of Irish guys back home have this tattoo and don't know it's the Notre Dame mascot.

Ollie was taking a couple hundred pills from me every week or so, and he seemed pretty reliable. He always had the money and was very eager. But I heard word that he had been caught dealing by the cops in the Carraig Springs nightclub. When I asked him about it, he said that it was no big deal. This should have been a red flag, but the drugs and alcohol that were helping me not to feel anything also made it difficult to think about anything. All the late nights and chemicals were wearing me out, and my head was rarely clear. So, when Ollie told me there was a big party happening in Cavan the next week and asked me to come up with everything I had, I missed that red flag too. If someone was just caught by the cops and they suddenly want more drugs than they ever got from you before, it's probably a setup. I had just bought a quarter kilo of speed and there were still a few ounces left of it, so I packed a duffel bag with the amphetamines and about a hundred ecstasy tablets and hopped on the bus that would take me from Dublin to Cavan.

I was already on edge that day. The night before, I'd had a nightmare in which I'd been caught by the cops. In my gut I had a bad feeling about this deal, but I was going ahead anyway. Ollie kept texting and calling me, asking, "Where are ya now?!" "Where are ya now!?" Another red flag. I was already feeling paranoid, so this heightened it. I may sound stupid for not getting off the bus and heading back to Dublin, but at the time I was just beaten. Dealing drugs requires you to be on full alert at all times, which is even harder when you're using them as well, and I was exhausted and sick from all the running around and ducking and diving. I thought, *Fuck it, if they're gonna catch me, they're gonna catch me.* Some shred of self-preservation told me not to get off at the Cavan bus station. I decided to get off one stop before, at the Meadow View restaurant, instead. Boy, was I smart. So smart that I told Ollie I would get off at the Meadow View.

I had barely stepped off the bus when the drug squad arrived. There was nowhere to run. The cops took the duffel bag and put the handcuffs on me. People in the parking lot looked on in shock—plainclothes detectives arresting bad guys right in front of their local establishment. The customers looked at me like I was a piece of shit. I had to agree with their opinion of me.

I was too tired to even try to put up a defense, so I admitted the drugs were mine. Even though my lawyer said this was extremely stupid, the judge took it into account and sentenced me to probation, no jail time. Being arrested and put on probation would be a wake-up call for most people, but not for me. It didn't change the way I lived. I just learned to be a little more careful. The following years brought more run-ins with the law, as well as too many beatings to count.

Sometimes we don't see the path we are on in life until later. What started with that innocent first beer getting me out of my head led to me being an alcoholic/bad boy. Deciding to keep it going, I had graduated to drugs and being a gangster. The initial goal was to get away from the fear and discomfort inside me, but at best they made me feel nothing. Being "Comfortably Numb" wasn't all it was cracked up to be and wasn't doing anything but pushing me deeper and deeper into a dark hole of depression and hopelessness.

At the twelve-step meetings, I was told I needed to find a higher power or I wouldn't be able to stay sober. If you believe in God and turn your life over to him, you are giving yourself over to a new higher power, and in return, gaining a feeling of peace and self-acceptance. With drugs and alcohol, they become your higher power, and the side effects are fear and coercion. Where God gives you free will, drugs and alcohol take it away. You're no longer in control. Throw in a life of crime and you have to watch out for anyone bigger, stronger, or crazier than you are. You're constantly living in fear of your life and looking over your shoulder. That was a feeling that stayed with me right up to the point I was about to blow my brains out and called Bernard.

And now I needed a higher power, but with God, alcohol, and drugs off the table, I had no idea where to turn.

I had taken the occasional stab at exploring other higher powers. Me and my buddy Chops used to fuck around with the Ouija board back in high school, and for a while I truly believed it was a link to people who had passed on. Chops would come over to my place and we would draw up a Ouija board like one he had seen in the encyclopedia. We would try to call up dead people like Kurt Cobain, Elvis Presley, and Adolf Hitler, or try to get the winning lottery numbers. The most that ever came up was three numbers. Not enough for the jackpot. And not enough to build a spiritual life around.

One night we did it and something weird happened that made me a believer. We had used a shot glass as the planchette, and when we were finished Chops went home. I put the glass into the dishwasher and went to bed. Teenagers tend to lock their bedroom door for obvious reasons, and I was no different. I locked my door, turned off the light, and went to sleep. When I woke up the next morning, the room was cold. My hair was standing on end. I got up and I saw that the glass we had been using for the Ouija board was on my desk! My door was still locked. So was the window. Nobody could have come in or out. It freaked the shit out of me. I got that glass, went outside, broke it, and buried it. I put holy water around the house where we had been using the Ouija board. I never did that shit again after that.

Even though I experimented with its power as a kid, I couldn't see myself as a grown man relying on a Ouija board to be the higher power that would keep me sober. But the people at the meetings told me I had to find something or I would be drinking and doing drugs in no time. They said it didn't have to be "God" or the "Jesus God" I was raised with. They said I could make up my own higher power. I just had to have something.

I hung out with this young Irish-American guy called Kevin, a tall junkie with a shamrock tattoo on his neck. He was one of these new dudes with no car who I picked up and brought to meetings regularly. When I told him I was having trouble finding a higher power, Kevin suggested that the group who goes to meetings with me could be my higher power. *Yes! That's a great idea!* The recovery group was a bunch of people who had figured out how to stay sober. Clearly, a power greater than me, because I hadn't figured that shit out. So the group became my higher power. Until Pat Maguire ruined the idea.

Pat was a cool Irish-American fella, a former gang member who had turned his life around. He had been the leader of this Irish gang that existed in San Francisco called SDI (Sunset District Irish). I had heard rumors that back in the nineties they used to grab Mexicans off the street, kidnap them in vans, paint them green, and let them out again. Pat assured me that this was bullshit. He would have these small daytime meetings at a friend's church on Taraval Street, and I would go and chat with the others about sobriety. At one of these meetings, I told Pat that the group was my higher power.

"That's a stupid higher power."

I immediately felt defensive. "No, it's not. Why do you say that?"

"Because if anything happens to the group you're fucked. What if they all go drink or die in a plane crash or something?"

Fuck. He was right. If something happened to the group, I had no higher power.

I had heard some old hippie say his higher power was a tree, so next I told Pat my new higher power would be a tree.

"If your higher power is a tree, I'll get my chainsaw, cut it down, and burn it with gasoline."

I was starting to get a bit annoyed. "Okay, what about a doorknob then?"

"If your higher power is a doorknob, I'll get my shotgun and blow your higher power away."

"Fuck, Pat, you're killing me. What higher power is safe from you?"

"Look. The best thing to have as a higher power is something you can't see. You don't even need to define it. All you need to know is that it's there. Then nothing can fuck with it. Something you can't see is the best higher power."

I let that sit with me for a while. It sort of made sense. Bernard told me I just needed to pray to this higher power every time I got a craving for booze or drugs. Or every time I had a problem or felt bad or worried about something or was angry. He said I just needed to go to this higher power and hand it over to them, to say, "I'm having these feelings, please help me."

So I tried, and to my own surprise, it started to work. Every time I got a craving for alcohol or drugs, I would pray to this higher power, whatever it was, and it killed the craving. And something else started to creep back into my life. A bunch of negative feelings I hadn't had in years. Resentments, fears, and regrets. Everything my substance abuse had kept away came flooding back in high definition. Some good, some bad, but feeling something was already feeling a whole lot better than feeling nothing.

It's weird because I still don't even know what my higher power is. All I know is that when I hit my knees and pray every morning and every night, I ask it to keep me sober. And it works. It's still bizarre to me. Something that I can't see or touch or define is actually keeping me sober.

The way I see it is there are two possibilities. One, this higher power is real, because it cured me of an incurable mental illness. Two, it's not real, but believing in it is, and taking these actions of prayer cured me of this incurable mental illness, like some sort of mindfuck. I don't question it much beyond that, because either way, it works.

STEP FOUR

THE SHIT LIST

**MAKE A SEARCHING
AND FEARLESS MORAL INVENTORY
OF YOURSELF**

THE GUY WHO LIVED NEAR me when I was seven.

Bank of America.

Australia.

These were the first three things I wrote down when I made up my shit list.

Step Four of the twelve steps is to Make a Searching and Fearless Moral Inventory of Yourself. That sounded intimidating at first, but when it was described to me as my shit list, where all I had to do was write down all the things that I hated or made me angry, I thought, *I can do that!* There were a lot of people, places, and things that pissed me off! It sounded grand, a lovely stroll down the memory lane of every grudge I had been nurturing all these years.

I was raring to go, but Bernard and the others in my group warned me not to take this one lightly, saying this was the step when a lot of people gave up and went drinking. That seemed crazy to me. This was about people who fucked *me* over. What could be so hard about writing that shit down? I was the victim! Actually, I thought it could be helpful to get some clarity about who was to blame for most of my behavior. So, off I went, confident I could get through my list quickly and without ending up at a bar or facedown in a pile of cocaine.

I figured I might as well start with the earliest one I could think of, so right at the top of my shit list was the guy who lived near me when I was seven. I couldn't remember his name at first. That was a little disconcerting, until I reasoned that it was because I was traumatized so badly that my mind had blocked it out. Anyway, I really hated his guts, this "guy who lived near me when I was seven." I was fooling around one day, chasing some horses in a field. I don't think the horses even belonged to the guy, but out of nowhere he threw me up against a gate and kicked me until I pissed myself. It totally caught me by surprise and was very traumatic. It hurt, but not as much as the embarrassment of having to deal with my soaked pants. I never forgot him. "If I ever meet the cunt again," I told Bernard, "I will break his fuckin' mouth." Twenty-one years after it happened, I was still furious about it. On the list he went. I was rolling. *Fuck these pricks who had fucked me over!* Okay, who was next? There were so many choices it was hard to narrow them down. I was actually having trouble focusing when Bank of America popped into my head.

Bank of America had ripped me off on some charges. It happened when I was in Rosarito, Mexico, and hooked up with these fine Mexican girls at Papas&Beer. They took me out drinking and to strip clubs, and at one point I went to the ATM with my Bank of America card to get more cash. The next morning, I noticed something interesting about my card. It was from Bank of America, but instead of "Richard Stephens" printed on the bottom, the name now read "Miguel Navarro."

What the fuck? Clearly, I had been played. I tried to contact B of A, but the challenge of completing an international call proved to be too much for my brain, which was still a bit foggy from the alcohol and drugs I had consumed. This meant I had to go back across the border to San Diego and cancel the card because I didn't want those girls to clear out my account. I finally made it to a Bank of America and discovered they'd stolen $500 from me! I think B of A said they were going to cancel the card and reverse the transaction, but I was still wasted on some Mexican pharmaceuticals I had scored down there, so I was never certain. Whatever the details were about those contested charges, there was one thing I was sure of: Bank of America had fucked me over and was going on my shit list. It was a very unpleasant experience all around, and I was sure they didn't try hard enough to make the bad feelings go away even if they made the charges go away. Actually, now that I thought of it, the Federales had chased me down there one night too. Jot that down. "Federales in Rosarito". *Fuckers.*

Then, I began having trouble with my list. I was getting agitated and edgy. I got up and started pacing. Maybe I needed to go for a run to clear my head. So, I did just that. It worked until I sat down to my list and all the agitation and edginess came back. I wanted to just get this damn thing done, so I thought for a moment and wrote: AUSTRALIA.

Australia was not the name of one of my stripper friends. And it wasn't like "the guy who lived near me when I was seven," a way of describing the person that did me wrong by their location. Nope, I meant the *country* of Australia. I had just put an entire country—maybe even a continent—on my shit list. Why not?

Before I almost blew my brains out, I moved to Melbourne. It was on January 1, 2010, and I was looking to start over the new year and the new decade in a new country. My life in San Francisco had become a nightmare. I was having serious problems with my wife; I told her I wasn't using drugs, but I was doing coke day and night and she was constantly complaining that I was high and lying to her about it. I also told her I had quit dealing, but she knew I had all kinds of money. And a gun. I told her I was a loan shark, but she wasn't really buying it. I decided to move in with my girlfriend, but things didn't get a whole lot better. More and more, coke just left me more and more depressed. I couldn't remember ever feeling so low. The economy sucked, but I heard things were booming in Australia. Suddenly, that seemed like the answer to all my problems. I would get out of town, get some work, clean myself up, and all would be grand.

My girlfriend really wanted to go with me, but I didn't care if we went together or not. I was only thinking about myself and needed to get away as fast as possible. She was an accountant and had to give notice before she could quit her job. I told her that I would go first and she could just meet me there in a couple of weeks. She pleaded, "No, let's go together."

There was no way I could wait, so I went online and started booking my tickets and visa for the soonest flight I could catch. My girlfriend saw what I was doing and went outside and turned off the internet! She told me some bullshit that raccoons or squirrels ate the cables and it would take the phone company a few days to fix it. I was super strung out on coke, so I'm sure she thought I would buy it, but I knew she was only keeping me there for those extra days so she could put in her final days at work. Actually, come to think of it, the girlfriend had to go down on the list, too—before Australia, because she had been the one stopping me from going there!

I thought about going to an internet café to buy the tickets, but I was so high that I couldn't leave the house. If I showed up anywhere in public, people would have called the cops on me. I was stuck, so my girlfriend's plan worked. We booked a flight together for New Year's Day. On Christmas Eve, I decided to kill myself.

My girlfriend had gone somewhere for Christmas. I was sitting in her house, drinking, doing cocaine, and feeling very sorry for myself. I was alone and full of regret. Nothing in my life was working out, and it seemed like it never would. I thought, *Fuck Australia, I'll just check out now instead.* I took out my gun, put a bullet in the clip, inserted the magazine, and cocked it. It was ready. I took a few more lines of coke, and I was ready. Then I decided to write a suicide note. If I was going to kill myself, I wanted it to be clear why I did it, the reasons I was so unhappy, and so the people who had fucked me over would know it was their fault. I got some printer paper and started writing. I was doing coke the whole time and wrote a few pages. I started to read it over, just to see if it sounded okay. It didn't. I can't really remember what it said, but it was absolute bullshit, pure gibberish. I thought *Fuck it, I can't leave this,* so I went into the bathroom and flushed it down the toilet.

I went back to the table, did some more coke, then picked up the gun and tried to steel myself to pull the trigger. My laptop was in front of me, and Facebook was open. A message popped up. (Yes, my girlfriend had restored the internet before she left. Merry Christmas!) My old college friend, Cole, had written, "Hey Richie. Happy Christmas!" I messaged him back, telling him that it was going to be my last, that I was now going to kill myself. My phone rang. It was him calling from Ireland, so I answered. I don't really remember a lot of the conversation, but I do remember telling him how low I felt and what my problems were, that there was no other way out, and it was all over. Cole was always a really smooth guy, too cool for school, the type of person who never gets rattled by anything. But whatever I said to him on the phone that day, he started crying. My bullshit had reduced him to tears. For some reason, hearing him like that snapped me out of my stupor. I didn't want to cause other people that kind of pain and upset. I put the gun away, left the coke out, and thought that I might just give Australia a chance to make this up to me. When my girlfriend came back, she had no idea what she'd missed.

Maybe Australia didn't have a chance considering the state I was in, but it sucked from day one. My girlfriend had pissed me off beyond repair by holding me hostage with the internet off, and I was fairly determined to be done with her. We checked into a hostel as soon as we arrived in Melbourne. It was the middle of the summer and unbelievably hot, like 120 degrees Fahrenheit. There was no sign of the cool ocean breezes I had been imagining.

One of the things the tourism bureau doesn't tell you about Australia is that drugs are super expensive compared to America—at least they were then. Coke was $250 a gram. Plus, it was really low-grade weak shit. I loved coke a lot but not enough to lay down 250 bucks. Even booze was stupidly expensive. A case of beer was nearly 60 bucks, and it was crap, with low alcohol content, 3 percent stuff, so I mostly drank this cheap boxed wine called "goon." It wasn't even made from grapes. If you read the box, it said it was made from fish bones and shit. But it was cheap, so I drank it.

The girlfriend and I split up, and I found a job working construction. I spent day after day sweating my ass off in the hot sun, and every night in the bars and legal whorehouses getting drunk and high and fist fighting. The only cheap drug there at the time was something called "mephedrone," an offshoot of MDMA that hadn't been made illegal yet. I lost a ton of weight. It didn't occur to me at the time, but my life hadn't changed, only the location had. At least in America people genuinely like the Irish. They think we are charming. That wasn't the case in Australia. A lot of immigrants were coming from Ireland at the time and I'm sure that caused tension with the Aussies. Irish and Aussies both like to drink and fight, so the fuse was already lit before we started taking what they saw as their jobs and their women. After a few months of shitty drugs, expensive booze, and hard labor in 120 degree heat, I was done. I never hated a place more. I returned to America and told everyone that Australia was the worst place on earth. I felt completely justified putting it on my shit list. I hated Australia, and I was pretty sure Australia hated me!

I went back to my list but couldn't seem to come up with anything for the next entry. There were just five things on there, and only three were actually people! I felt like shit and was having a lot of trouble digging deeper into my memories. Drunks and addicts don't dwell on the past. Oh, we'll use a recent slight or an old disappointment to justify more drinking and doing drugs, but we are not the types to look too hard in the rearview mirror. To remember means putting your life in focus, and that's a hard thing for a substance abuser to do. The past is full of things that you know are going to make you feel bad, and if you're not completely motivated to change your life, there's a good chance it will trigger you to start using again. It's easier to just forget the past.

The wall I had hit made me suddenly realize something: A lot of the stuff that was pissing me off was in the present. The here and now. Work, my wife, the guys in the group—it seemed like everyone and everything needed to go on my shit list. It was unrelenting and all-encompassing. I scrawled all those things down, and as I looked at the list I realized just how angry I was. Not even at a specific person or wrongdoing. I was just angry.

This really shook me. I thought when I got over the cravings to drink and do drugs, everything would seem brighter and more hopeful. But that was far from true. I would walk around town day after day, as agitated or pissed off as I had always been, but now I didn't have booze or weed or coke to turn to for comfort.

As much as drugs and alcohol turn your life upside down, cutting them out of your life is no picnic either. Before I got sober, most of my waking thoughts had been about when I would have my next drink, when I could score more drugs or the things that happened the last time I did them. The people I hung out with were people I drank or got high with. The places I went to were places I could drink or do drugs. And now those people and places had to be out of my life. I had stirred up all these feelings that I had worked so hard to keep away, but how could I get rid of this anger? The boys at the meetings told me that addiction was a disease of selfishness, so in order to get rid of that, we had to help others. I had just finished my career as a drug dealer, so, barely into Step Four, I decided I was going to try to convert my old clients.

I went around to my customers to tell them I was done using drugs, that the twelve-step program was amazing and that they should go to the meetings too. Yes, I had just been selling drugs to them a few weeks before, but now I was coming back with a positive message of hope that they would never get from another dealer. One of the first people I tried to convert was Tom the Gardener. He lived near my house and we were buddies from my local bar, the Hockey Haven. He was a gardener for the city and one of my best customers. Maybe one of the reasons I liked him so much was that his coke habit was so much worse than mine. I would go to his house and think, *This poor fucker REALLY has a problem.* He was so bad with his habit that I actually felt guilty about giving him stuff and had warned him that if he didn't cut down, I would stop selling to him.

He rang me looking for coke, and I called round to him and said, "Dude. There's these meetings and you go there and they teach you how to not get high! It's great. Let's do it!"

He looked at me like I had lost my mind and said, "Nah. That's okay. I don't have a problem, I can stop any time I want. You go to your meetings. It'll be good for you."

It was the same with my other customers. You can tell someone they have cancer and they will find every treatment they can to help themselves get better, but if you tell someone they have a drinking or drug problem, they refuse to believe it. I couldn't understand how these people didn't get it the same as I did. They thought what I was doing was crazy. But it was so clear to me. I went one time and pretty much figured out I was in the right place. It was weird because something had switched in my brain and I wanted to help the other people who were fucked up like me. But why wouldn't they listen? Part of it is that druggies won't listen until the time is right. That is the part about hitting rock bottom. But the other part was that they might have seen it as just plain ridiculous that their coke dealer was becoming righteous with them about the evils of Uncle Charlie.

When I quit dealing, I had to tell my suppliers, Ronald and Leroy, that I wasn't going to be getting any more coke from them. I called Ronald to tell him I was trying to be sober and didn't want anything to do with buying or dealing drugs, but he wanted to meet face-to-face. Even though I always paid cash and there was never any money owed or those kinds of fuck-ups, I still felt a little worried when he told me he wanted to meet. Before this, we had always just talked on the phone. Was I about to get one in the back of the head? I knew if I didn't show up for the meeting I definitely would. I had been reliable, honest, and trustworthy with them, so all I could do was show up and hope for the best.

We met up the next Saturday in the Richmond District. Ronald got into my truck and shut the door. Things were tense. This is the moment when I would be getting shot if that was going to happen. "Champagne Supernova" was playing on the radio. Ronald remarked that he "was all about Oasis." This calmed my nerves a little. I reiterated what I had told him on the phone, and Ronald said, "I'm happy for you. You're a good guy and if you have a problem you're doing the right thing." Ronald was always sober when I met him as he didn't like to dabble in his product. I told him he was always decent with me, I was just done with the business. He said he respected that, but that if I wanted to give him my customers, he would compensate me. I wouldn't even need to meet them or touch the stuff, he would just buy my customers and give me money every week. As tempting as that was, and even though I wouldn't need to see anyone or touch any-thing, I couldn't do it.

I told him that if any of my former customers called looking for stuff, I would pass them to him and he didn't need to give me anything. He still wanted to pay me, but I couldn't take that money in good conscience. I just wouldn't feel right about it. He asked if I was sure—it was free money, a residual income—but I thanked him for the offer and said no. The funny thing was, after this, all the old people who used to buy coke off me didn't want to buy it off him. I told them he was a really cool guy, reliable and trustworthy, but they just didn't want to meet him. They were scared. This didn't make any sense to me. If I found a good coke connection, I would keep it, dangerous or not. But I guess that's why I'm an addict, not a casual user.

After cutting ties with all my customers and suppliers, the circle of people I came into contact with had changed. Now it was mostly sober people. A lot of them were on my shit list. I had stopped drinking and doing drugs; I had found a higher power and put my illegal affairs behind me. And yet I was still pissed off and angry. Weren't those feelings supposed to go away?

This was when I first heard the phrase "dry drunk." Just because your higher power keeps you from drinking, it doesn't mean you're sober. You still have many of the traits of an alcoholic, just without the drinking. *Well fuck me,* I thought, *what's the point of even doing all this?* I could start to understand why so many people started drinking again at this step. All the bad feelings were brought to the surface, and you had no medicine to help you through it. It was awful.

Around this time, I met an old Irish guy called John. He was sober for a long time. He asked me what "step" I was on.

"I'm trying to get through the fourth step."

"What do you mean you're trying to do it? You're either doing it or you're not."

I told him I was slowly doing it, and he looked me right in the eye and said, "Well get it done or you'll die like a dog in the street." It was not preachy. He didn't flinch when he said it. It was not comforting. It was a statement of fact, and it got to me like only a simple truth can.

I went straight home and started working on the list. Walter made it for ratting me out about the IDs. Ollie for setting me up with the cops. It felt good to write it all down. I remember having heard that Ollie was in New York and I had seriously thought about having him whacked for what he did to me. Now, it all just felt like water under the bridge. I finished the list and I felt like I had done something important. I was less edgy. I was less angry.

Step Four had been as difficult as they said. Denial is such a huge part of alcoholism and drug addiction; dredging into the depths of my dark past, and being forced to analyze the things I had buried for years was one of the hardest things I've done. It forced me to completely rethink the vision I had of myself. Only my belief that I would "die like a dog in the street" kept me from giving up. But I had completed my list and I felt pretty good. I was very capable of writing down the list of people who had fucked me over and what they had done to me, but there was a final column that mostly remained blank when I was writing.

It said: "What was your part in all of it?"

STEP FIVE

MAYBE I'M NOT SUCH A GOOD GUY...

—◈—

ADMIT TO GOD, YOURSELF, AND ANOTHER THE NATURE OF YOUR WRONGS

—◈—

WHEN YOU SPEND ALL YOUR time with drinkers and drug users, you're bound to hear about someone "working the steps." It might be about a missing drinking buddy ("You didn't hear? Jimmy is working the steps") or a customer who declines when you offer them some prime coke ("Don't call me anymore, Richie. I'm working the steps"). Even when I started going to meetings and the veterans constantly told me to just "work the steps," I thought "work" was just another way to say "do." I had committed to getting sober. The hard part was done, now I just had to do the steps. Clearly, I had underestimated things. Step Four had been a real challenge, but I made it through and got my shit list done. Step Five was all about sharing that shit list with my sponsor and talking about it. This forced me to look within myself in a way I had never dared, and made it possible to look at things with a perspective I couldn't see before.

After my first few meetings, I thought that the people who were there in the room would always be around. We'd all decided to quit drinking and doing drugs, and I figured we'd celebrate our sober anniversaries together. But soon I noticed that people would disappear. Many of them would really "talk the talk," and seemed to be working the program and staying sober, but it turned out they were secretly using all the time. I saw it over and over again and just couldn't understand it. What was the point of pretending? If you want to drink, just go and fucking do it. What's the point of coming to meetings and trying to fool people? Who cares? Then I remembered that I had played these charades myself when I was younger and on probation.

I was pretending to get help with a problem I didn't really believe I had so everyone would get off my back.

Other people would suddenly just snap. They would go out drinking and do something crazy like try to make the cops kill them. I started to sit in the back of the room at meetings and try to guess who was going to fall off the wagon. It was a weird thing to do, kind of arrogant I guess, but in my head, I would always try to pick the losers.

One night I pointed out some guy to Bernard and said, "Look at this fucker. He's never going to make it. He's never gonna get it."

Bernard looked me dead in the eye and said, "Don't ever fuckin' make fun of these cunts. That could be *you*. *You* could relapse and be the same as them."

Bernard told me that instead of trying to pick out the losers, I needed to find the winners and stick with them. "The winners are the people who are really trying to do the right thing and stay sober. They are doing the work. These are the people you need to stay with if you're going to make it."

But how could you tell who these "winners" were? It took a while, but I realized there was one key factor that set them apart: They were honest and really participated in what was going on—not being tourists like the ones who kept on relapsing.

When writing out my shit list, I felt unsettled, as promised by the others who had been through it. Now, I had to meet with Bernard and talk about it. This had really worried me, but looking down at my list, it didn't seem so hard. I had always believed I was unlucky, so most issues I had weren't my fault, and the list just reinforced that idea. When I sat down with Bernard to go over it, I figured it wouldn't take long. One of the first ones I told him about was Ollie and how he was on there because he ratted me out.

"What was your part in it?"

"Nothing," I said. "I'm a stand-up guy, I never snitched on anyone. The cops said I wouldn't even have to go to court if I ratted on my supplier."

"But you were selling drugs."

"Yeah. So?"

"That's illegal. If you weren't dealing, he couldn't have told on ya."

Huh. Good point, Bernard. Maybe I needed to take a closer look at my list.

A guy named Jon Stack was a top-ten entry. We used to go out drinking together when I was on probation after being set up by Ollie. From the time I was sixteen, my practice had been to use drugs to "balance me out" when I was drinking. But while on probation I had to have random drug tests, so I didn't risk using. This led to me being a pretty bad drunk. One night, Jon and I were knacker drinking in Cavan, in the parking lot beside the cinema. A few proper dirtbags from the Half Acre were there too. I was a sloppy drunk and I'm sure pretty obnoxious as well. I was talking shit about Ollie, calling him a rat and a few worse things for setting me up with the cops. I can remember one of the other guys saying he was Ollie's cousin, but this didn't stop me and I only got more belligerent. Jon tried to settle me down, but there was no controlling me, and he finally said he wasn't in the mood for listening to my bullshit and left me there alone with them.

All I remember after Jon left was that someone hit me over the head with a wine bottle, smashing it. Then they hopped the living shit out of me, beat me unconscious, and left me for dead. I don't know how long I was there, but it must have been four or five hours. I woke up covered in blood and glass. My phone was gone. My wallet was gone. They had broken my front tooth as well.

I ended up in the hospital for a few days because there was blood in my urine from being repeatedly kicked and punched in the kidneys. All I could think about was how angry I was at Jon. He was a big dude, and there was no way they would have taken the two of us on in a fair fight. I was only in the hospital pissing blood and missing a tooth because he'd abandoned me.

Bernard didn't have to tell me my part in that one. The scumbags from the Half Acre might have thrown the punches, but if I hadn't been drunk and running my mouth I wouldn't have ended up in hospital. It all started with me.

Names from my list started swimming in my mind. So many of them looked different with this new perspective, and it was incredibly difficult to face the fact that a lot of the grudges I held against others were at least partly my fault. All along, I had been sure that I was really a good guy, so it became very important for me to find examples where I was the clear victim. There had to be at least one! I thought Connolly was my answer.

In 2007, I was overseeing a construction job in Berkeley. One morning I showed up to find someone had driven off with a bunch of washing machines that had been left in the courtyard. The security guard who was supposed to be watching the place was nowhere to be found. I called the cops and reported the theft. That should have been it. Next thing I know, though, Connolly, the contractor who oversaw installation of metal plates on the building, told my boss I was behind the robbery. My boss, Jerry, was one tough motherfucker so this put me in a dangerous spot. He wouldn't have reported me to the cops; he would have taken care of me personally. I couldn't believe Connolly would accuse me of such a thing, and I was furious that this little prick would endanger my name and my health by saying I had organized the robbery. He had to pay. I was going to beat his fucking ass.

I heard that Connolly lived in Vacaville, which was halfway to Sacramento, fifty-four miles away to be exact. No problem, I had a truck. I drank a couple of beers, got some cocaine, and called my friend Amos and told him we were going to beat this motherfucker. Amos was always up for my shenanigans, so I picked him up and handed him a fifth of whisky, gave him some coke, and we hit the road.

On the way, I explained to Amos what had happened and why "we" all of a sudden were going to hop Connolly. This guy had talked shit about me and now I was gonna kick his ass. Amos kept saying, "This is stoopid. This is stoopid." I told him to shut the fuck up, drink his whiskey, and snort his coke. I don't really know why I even brought Amos. Connolly was a little fucker. I could have put him in hospital with one hand tied behind my back. I guess I just wanted company.

We arrived in Vacaville and...I realized I had no idea where Connolly lived. Vacaville is a pretty big place so knocking on doors was out of the question. I rang my buddy Francie, who worked for Connolly and hated him as much as I did.

"Francie, where does this motherfucker live?"

"Eh, I know how to get there, but I don't know what the address is."

Fuck sake. "Can you describe it to me?"

Francie described the road it was on and said it was near the water. When I asked for more details, Francie said, "Eh, why don't ya just call Connolly and ask him for the address?" I told Francie it wasn't exactly a social call. Silence for a few seconds. Then he told me to give Connolly a few clouts from him while I was at it.

I tried to follow Francie's directions as best I could. We drove out to the road he told us to, but there were a bunch of houses by the water and I couldn't figure out which one it was. Francie told me there was a boat outside the house, but loads of houses had boats out front. Next, I tried calling Francie's son, Derek, who also worked for Connolly. Same shit with Derek. He didn't know the address but knew how to get there and kind of described it. The state that I was in with the booze and coke didn't help either. I just couldn't find it. In the end, we had to give up. We drove back to San Francisco in silence. Amos was right. It was stupid.

When I finished telling Bernard this one, he stared at me a moment. "So what happened? What did your boss do to you?"

"Nothing. Jerry had asked my friend, Arthur, 'Did that tick cunt organize the robbery?' and Arthur said, 'Nah. He's too stupid to organize a robbery.' Then Jerry said, 'I was thinking that myself.' Case closed."

"So you never got in trouble? Did you kick this Connolly's arse?"

"Nah. I was going to hop him at a jobsite on another day but Arthur sent me home before I could get to him. But you're missing the point, Bernard, I had no blame in this. That prick accused me of a crime I didn't commit."

Bernard looked at me, stumped. It felt like I really had him this time. Then he said, "Why do you suppose he did that?"

"I don't know." But as soon as the words left my mouth, I did know. A few days earlier, the copper company had dropped off a bunch of boxes that were meant for somewhere else. I told Francie about it and said the company was going to come back and get them. He asked "Why don't we take some?" We could cut them up and sell them for scrap. They were really expensive, and we could pocket a few hundred dollars per box. I figured they didn't belong to our employers or the property owner so we were taking them from the supplier, which didn't seem wrong to me. We put a few boxes each in our vehicles, but one of the other workers saw us and told Connolly we were stealing from the job. I suppose it didn't take a huge leap on Connolly's part to think I was in on the other robbery as well.

After realizing I had played a big part in this grudge too, the floodgates opened and I told Bernard story after story where I had felt wronged and now realized my part in it. He would listen and in his gruff voice say, "Yeah, that's the same shit. You don't have to tell me that." But there was no stopping me.

There was a very good reason I was rolling with these stories. They kept me from confronting the really hard ones. I now had no problem admitting a lot of my grudges came from my drinking or using or dealing drugs. What I didn't want to have to admit was that a lot of the people closest to me, people I still resented, were people I had wronged in a much deeper, more hurtful way. People who suffered because of my selfishness.

Addicts are fragile, and selfishness is an act of self-preservation. Like a house of cards that will collapse if one is removed, the narrative of why they are entitled to keep drinking and doing drugs would fall apart if an addict stopped to think of others, paused to recognize the hurt they were doing to those closest to them. I didn't want to go deeper and examine my selfishness. There was something dark and painful lurking there that I didn't want to confront. But if I didn't want to be one of the losers, I had to.

My wife was on my shit list. We met when I was twenty-two and she was thirty-two, and soon after we started dating she got pregnant. She asked me if I would marry her, and I said no. I felt like she had gotten the chance to enjoy her youth and now she was trying to take mine away. I began to resent her for putting me in this position. She cried for three days, and I finally agreed to marry her, thinking it was "the right thing to do." The selfish part of me, though, felt like since I did the right thing, it was fair for me to keep on doing what I had been doing—drinking, drugs, and sleeping with other women.

I never even thought about what all this behavior must be doing to her. Why would I? I was the victim here, so anything I did was justified. So many times, she would call me at four or five o'clock in the morning, wondering where I was, if I was even alive. These calls were always sure to wreck my buzz—I always had to come up with a new lie just to get her off my back. I couldn't just let the phone ring out. It was torture.

One night, while I was wasted with my buddy, Halton, she called and said, "Where the fuck are you?!"

I was speechless. The first thing that came into my head was, "I got beat up."

"What?!"

I repeated it. She asked if I was okay, and I told her I got nailed with a few punches but I was okay and would be home soon. I hung up the phone and immediately realized I had told her I got beat up but wasn't actually beaten up. For the story to look true, I was going to need to get a few punches thrown at me. Halton was an amateur boxer, so there was no way I was letting him do it. I didn't want a broken jaw. There was only one thing for it. So, sitting on the couch in Halton's condo, I began punching myself in the face. Halton sat watching me, not understanding what was going on, but I kept at it until a good five or six marks were on my cheeks and around my eyes.

I had found myself in a position where I had to kick my own ass just so I could party and not go home to my wife and kid. And it was all her fault. Until I started working Step Five and realized it was all me.

As the fog in my head cleared, I began to properly evaluate my past experiences, with Bernard's help, showing me the things I had missed. The realization of how things had really happened began to sink in. I had avoided dealing with the actual truth for all these years. Resentments, fears, and regrets are things that keep an addict using. They get you feeling depressed and the end result is either drinking or getting high. These negative specifics had to be processed honestly in order for me to stay sober.

I looked back at my list. Now, I could see how I played a part in every grudge I'd had. No one made me drink or deal drugs, steal, or even get married. I had chosen every single one of those things. Even the few things that actually weren't my fault in any way, I played a part in; I was the one who chose to hold on to the resentment for so long.

A lot of the shit I was angry about from my life didn't disappear overnight. Some things took a while and I had to pray for them to be removed. But once I accepted my role in it all, I stopped feeling like a victim. A weight had been lifted off my shoulders. I actually felt like I had some control in life. Since I had been the one to choose all those negative things, I could choose the positive things. I could choose to be one of the winners and stay sober.

STEP SIX

STOP BEING SUCH A BOLLOCKS

—◈—

**BECOME READY
TO LOSE THOSE DEFECTS**

—◈—

DRUGS ARE FUN. SORRY, BUT it's true.

I may have been a bad drunk—I once headbutted my best friend Brian at an office Christmas party because…well, I don't know why—but I could be entertaining as hell when I was high. Even though I sold a lot of drugs, I gave away a bunch too, and that made me a pretty popular guy. My associates in the drug-taking world, my very loyal customers, were always happy to see me. The day the Queen Mother died, my friends Divey and Carlo were having a big celebration in some shitty bar in Maynooth because somehow they saw her death (from natural causes) as a Republican victory. I walked in to sell them ecstasy, and they lit up like kids on Christmas morning. It actually made me feel really good about myself. *I'm Santa Claus for grown-ups!* Getting out of my own head and killing fear drove me to substance abuse, but a big part of what kept me going was how much fun I was having.

In 2004, I partnered up with my pal Ross to become a one-stop shop for people who wanted to party. He sold weed and I sold the ecstasy and coke, so we could supply everything everybody needed for a fun night out. We were friendly faces, knew lots of people, and went to parties where we would spend all night talking shit, drinking, smoking weed, and doing ecstasy with our customers. Like Julie the Cruise Director from *The Love Boat* (a show I was addicted to as a wee lad), it was our responsibility to keep everyone entertained. One game I came up with was "coke racing." I would make a couple of foot-long lines of coke side by side, and two people would compete against each other to see who could finish their line fastest. Ready, steady, snort. Whoever crossed the "finish line" first was the winner, and was awarded an ecstasy pill as their prize.

Even when working the shittiest jobs, like moving furniture in San Francisco, I mostly remembered the fun we had getting fucked up. A lot of Irishmen worked as movers in the States, and I had heard that this one Irish moving company was the best to work for because they would all do coke if the move involved stairs. That turned out to be untrue. They did coke for every move. Stairs or not. Anyone can do blow off a mirror, but I did lines off everything from antique desks to baby grand pianos. One of the moving truck drivers, a guy named Will, was a crackhead. When we were at the customer's house, he would crouch inside one of those wardrobe boxes and smoke the crack pipe. Sorry if your clothes smelled a little funky, but nothing was going to get moved without the help of all the drugs we did.

When I started to get sober and thought about these good times, I freaked out at the idea that I would never get high again. What about my sex life? Many nights when I was coked up, I could fuck whatever woman I was with more times than I could count (well, except one night when I counted nine times, a personal record; I was twenty-two and she was the forty-eight-year-old girlfriend of the guy who owned the local liquor store).

Step Six is all about preparing yourself to shed your character defects. After five grueling steps, I suddenly wasn't sure I was ready. My defects of character were what kept me safe. They were my self-preservation. Was I really never going to get high or have another drink for as long as I lived? All those days. All those hours. All those minutes. All those fucking seconds. Doing it for that long tripped me out and overwhelmed me.

I asked Bernard, "How the fuck am I supposed to do this shit?! I can't have a drink at my daughter's wedding twenty years from now?! If my parents die, how will I not drink?"

"Never mind that shit. You only think about it one day at a time. Fuck tomorrow. Only think about today. Fuck next year. Fuck whenever ya have a wedding. You just think about today. Today you're not gonna drink.

Worry about tomorrow when tomorrow happens. Maybe tomorrow you won't want to drink again as well. Okay?"

Thinking about it that way made it seem way less daunting. I could probably figure out one day of not drinking. *Okay, I guess I'm ready then...*

But was I really? I honestly didn't know. Because there were times before this when I thought I was ready to get sober and was very wrong.

Meeting Tabitha was one of those times. She was my dream girl. We met around the start of my second year at university. She was a couple of years older than me, and was absolutely gorgeous. Tall with black hair, she had Italian/Greek-type looks that were exotic for Ireland. She was popular too, and every guy wanted to be with her.

Tabitha and I "met cute." She liked ecstasy, and I was firmly established as a drug dealer. For drug addicts that counts as cute. A true storybook romance. I flirted with her a lot when I sold to her and she did it right back. I couldn't get her out of my head. Ferret told me, "If you can score with Tabitha, I will personally get you a trophy with your name on it!" That's how hard he thought it would be for me to date her. Whether it was the drugs or my sparkling personality, I didn't know and I didn't care, but Tabitha and I started going out, and before I knew it I was in love.

I had never been in love before. I'd had a bunch of relationships, but I never thought I was capable of actually loving anyone until I started taking ecstasy. I could be a pretty cold individual, closed off to a lot of emotion, but ecstasy opened me up, and I found I could care about a woman more deeply than I ever could in the past.

My time with Tabitha was probably the happiest I'd ever experienced. All I cared about was spending time with her...and partying, but those were not in conflict. I didn't even bother going to class, and pretty soon I had gotten so far behind that it felt like a waste of time to even bother with school. I just figured I'd give up, maybe repeat the year. Or not. From listening to Tommo, I started to develop an ambition for the criminal world, thinking, *Fuck school, I'm good at this, might as well keep at it because it's my best chance to become successful at something.*

Then, Tabitha grew tired of me. I was doing plenty of drugs so I was still fun (at least I thought so) but she felt our relationship wasn't going any-where—I wasn't going anywhere—and she dumped me. It was devastating. I wanted to be with her forever and felt really hurt and used. Ecstasy stretches your emotions. When you're happy, you're really, really happy, and when you're low, you're really fucking low. I sank into a deep depression.

One night, in a stupor, I decided I was going to commit suicide by jumping into the canal, even though it was only about four feet deep. For some reason, I thought I could drown myself in there. I remember speaking to Tommo on the phone, and him somehow talking me out of it. "Mush. Don't be stupid. In six months ya won't even remember this bitch." He got through to me. I decided not to kill myself. Until a few days later when, with the help of ecstasy, I reached a new depressive low.

I had gotten two bottles of Jack Daniel's, planning to drink myself into oblivion. The more I drank, though, the more it made sense to end it all. Life had become a dead end with no chance of improvement, and I just didn't want to deal with it anymore. I believed I had damaged my brain to the point of no repair with drugs, my college career was down the drain, and the woman I loved no longer wanted me. There was no friendly direc-tion and no hope. I was sure my life was ruined forever. I told myself, "Fuck it, let's do it."

I began swallowing loads of ecstasy. First a handful of five in one go, then more at regular intervals. I was smoking cigarettes and putting them out on my arm, to burn myself and feel the pain. I took a knife and carved the palm of my hand. These scars remain, running all the way up my left arm. I swallowed more and more ecstasy, and later figured I took about thirty pills, and had another seventy ready to go. Things were blurry but I remember shitting my pants and not caring. Soon enough that was going to be somebody else's mess to worry about. My friend Travis (who, FYI, I will fuck over later) came in and found me like that. I planned to keep on going until I was dead, but when I wasn't paying attention Travis took the remaining pills and hid them. When the pills were gone, I just decided to keep on drinking. Somehow, I lived, and no ambulance or police had to be called.

With two failed suicide attempts under my belt, I *was* ready to make a change, but not for the better. I decided I needed to up my game, so I called Tommo and asked if he could get me some heroin.

"Mush, what do ya want heroin for?"

"I want to kill myself."

Maybe this wasn't the smartest answer because he refused. "No. I'm not giving ya heroin. Cop yourself on."

"You don't understand. Tabitha left me and I don't know what to do."

Tommo told me to grab a taxi and come stay with him a while. On the ride, I wondered how I had gotten to such a desperate place. Maybe it was time to quit the booze and drugs. I remember feeling that this shit couldn't continue. Halfway to his place, I made a decision. I no longer wanted to end my life. But I wasn't ready to end my way of life either. I could begin to picture living without Tabitha, but I couldn't imagine a day-to-day existence without partying. I had the taxi driver turn around and went back to drinking and doing more and more ecstasy.

Since I was dealing ecstasy, I was able to afford them more than somebody who wasn't, because I got them in bulk for a discount. The thing with ecstasy, as with most drugs, is the more you take, the more your tolerance goes up. The longer you do it, the more serotonin gets depleted from your brain. Serotonin allows you to experience joy. So you're taking the same number of pills, but the feeling isn't as good because there is less serotonin to be released. Within one year of having started doing ecstasy, I would need to take between ten and twenty pills per night just to get the same buzz I had when I first tried it. Near the end of my ecstasy use, I would be gagging even trying to swallow one. My body was screaming for me to stop!

But my mind was stronger. I was actually proud of the fact that I could power through and keep doing drugs. If I could overcome my body telling me to stop, I figured I could quit whenever I was ready.

One time in 2006, after doing cocaine at the Hockey Haven, I got on the last Muni bus in a really positive, happy mood. No one else was on the bus and I was feeling chatty, so I sat up front beside the driver and started conversing. He was a big dude, a bit older than me. He asked me where I was from and I told him. He asked how long I had been in America and I told him that too. He asked if I had any kids and I said yes. All of a sudden, the conversation took a nosedive. We had been friendly and getting to know each other, but now he looked at me with disgust and asked, "Why are you doing this to yourself?"

That fucking froze me. It felt like a dagger. Up until that point I hadn't realized he knew I was high. I thought he just believed I was being friendly. But he had just met me and was calling me on my bullshit. I thought I was in a really good place. I worked, I helped support my wife and kids, and I knew how to have a good time with my friends. But this question, "Why are you doing this to yourself?" totally rocked me. I just kind of shrugged and pretended I didn't know what he meant. Then he dropped it. The conversation was over.

But that question fucked with me. Why did I keep doing this to myself when so many other people would have stopped? I didn't know the answer so I tried to forget it, told myself my high for the night was ruined, but there was always tomorrow. And thousands of tomorrows after that one. Because as low as I felt that night, I still wasn't ready.

Before I went to my first twelve-step meeting, I used to watch *Celebrity Rehab*. I would laugh at the contestants, thinking, *Ha! These clowns can't handle their shit!* I really thought I was better than them. Even though I was a fucking mess, I thought they were fools and that things were under control for me. After my suicide attempts, I still believed I was a tough, self-sufficient guy who could not only handle his shit, but could handle giving up his shit.

After starting the meetings, I still felt tough. No, I couldn't stop on my own, but I was confident I could stop with the help I was getting from the group. Conquering each difficult step made me think I was strong enough to make it. I was pretty proud of myself. I was going to be one of the winners.

The more I thought about this, the less worried I became that this time would be like those others. They were all in my past. I had made the commitment to come to meetings, work the steps, and do whatever it took to get sober. I'd come this far; I could keep going. *Okay, I'm definitely ready...*

When I told Bernard I was ready, I said, "I did all the steps so far. I'm not angry anymore. I took my part in any grudges I had. I'm being honest and doing the meetings and I'm committed."

Bernard looked concerned.

"What? What am I missing?"

"That's a lot of I's."

And that was the problem. To Become Ready is very different from being ready to quit drinking and drugs. Bernard told me that in order for me to Become Ready, I had to change in a dramatic, fundamental way; a whole new moral code was needed. As hard as it had been to admit I had a problem and seek help, I now had to do something even harder: I had to completely humble myself and become a different person. Drugs allowed me to let myself go; what I needed to do now was to let My Self go.

All religions teach about the dangers of selfishness, and that the path to happiness starts with losing oneself, giving oneself over. You can do this through prayer, meditation, or even just helping others. That always sounded like bullshit to me. But when you are only concerned with yourself, you feel the need to always be happy, which is a recipe for disaster. The path to happiness for me had always been partying—at least I thought it had. Looking back, though, I realized that whatever pleasure it brought was fleeting. There was always a crash after the high, never a feeling of being fulfilled. It was like scooping water into a bucket with a hole in it.

I had been raised around the Catholic Church, and had lived in San Francisco long enough to be exposed to every kind of hippie-dippy, do-gooder spiritual belief. This idea of putting others first seemed impossible to me. Everything people do is for themselves. I didn't think helping old ladies across the street or tossing money in a homeless person's cup was going to suddenly make me a better, less selfish person. I'd only be doing it because Bernard told me to, because I wanted to get sober.

Bernard usually had good explanations about the steps, but when I told him about my doubts that I could ever be truly selfless no matter how many people I helped, he said, "Don't think about it, just do it." He said I should start by helping some of the new guys.

"Bernard, I only have a few weeks of sobriety, I don't know jack shit about it yet."

"If you've got a few weeks, you can help someone who only has a few days. Just call them up and ask them how they're doing. Teach them the shit that you've learned already. Ask them to come to a meeting with you. If they have no car, fucking pick them up and take them to meetings."

Without much confidence in it working, I started trying to help others. I would go up to new guys, introduce myself, ask if they needed any help. Most of the guys obviously felt as uncomfortable about it as I did. Clearly, I wasn't a natural at this. Driving people to meetings seemed like something I could do; if things got too awkward I could always turn up the music. So, I became the guy who tried to drive people to meetings. I probably even became weirdly aggressive about it. One time I asked Kevin if he wanted a lift to the meeting and he told me he had developed agoraphobia (a fear of going outside). "Bullshit. I'll be over for ya in twenty minutes."

But a lot of the guys had lost their licenses to DUIs or lost their cars because the money went to drugs and alcohol instead of their monthly payments, so someone always needed a ride. I'm not sure I even noticed it, but I slowly stopped worrying about what we would talk about on the drive and started worrying that everyone who needed a ride would get one. The "I, I, I" that had been the main focus of my life had shifted, and the welfare of others grew in importance. Getting out of my own head had been my goal all along, and now I was experiencing it in a completely new and unexpected way. Helping others became an end in itself, and doing these actions helped to smooth out the old character defects.

I don't think I changed my moral code; helping others changed me. Lying and cheating and fighting, which had been second nature to me, became unappealing. They weren't the traits of the person I wanted to be, the model I wanted the new guys in the group to see and try to follow.

Everything I had done in my long life of partying, and my short few weeks of trying to get sober, was about me. Now, I was putting others first. I had Become Ready to shed those old selfish defects of character.

GOD, COULD YOU PLEASE HELP ME TO STOP BEING SUCH A BOLLOCKS?

HUMBLY ASK HIGHER POWER TO REMOVE YOUR DEFECTS

MELBOURNE, 2010.

IT'S ONE OF MY FIRST nights in Australia, and I'm drunk. The girlfriend and I have been drinking in a bar for a while and, go-getter that I am,
I've already figured out a money-making scam. This is how it works: The
Australian government was paying homeowners to change the insulation
in their houses to more modern energy-efficient stuff. The whole idea was
to save money on electricity, heating, and air conditioning, plus help the
environment. To do the scam, you rent a van for the day, pick up some
bales of insulation, and report to the assigned homeowner. They let you in,
and you go up into their attic space and pretend to change out the old insulation. Basically, you just fuck around up there a while, use a broom to tap
the ceiling joists so it sounds like you're working, but you don't change the
original insulation, you just leave it up there and keep the new stuff in your
van. No one is going up to check the "work," it's over a hundred degrees
Fahrenheit up there in the summer. The homeowner pays you, and then
later you sell the bales that you got at the start of the day to someone else.

Some other drunk with an entrepreneurial spirit similar to mine had
told me about the scam, and now I'm telling it to a new drinking buddy, a
traveler dude from England who is also visiting Australia. While I'm chatting with him, this big, chubby Australian guy comes into the bathroom
where we are conducting our business meeting and says, "Hey, no gay shit
in here!" I feel my blood begin to boil. *Who is this asshole and why is he giving
me shit, interrupting my business meeting? He knows I'm not gay because he saw
me with my girlfriend, but he's trying to provoke me anyway, playing Billy Big*

Bollocks. He means it as an insult and thinks I won't do anything about it because he's about a hundred pounds heavier than me.

"Fuck off," I tell him, spoiling for a fight, but the guy wisely turns and walks out. *That's that,* I think, and my heartrate slows. Back at the bar, though, while I'm talking to my girlfriend, I see the guy out of the corner of my eye. He's talking to someone and pointing at me. They're both giving me dirty looks from across the bar. The anger comes flooding back, and I turn to my girlfriend and say, "I'm going to nail this prick." I give her my phone and wallet to hold onto, in case I get arrested, then walk over to the guy and tap him on the shoulder.

"What the fuck were you saying?"

He responds, "I'm from Queensland, me."

His buddies laugh.

"I don't care where the fuck you're from. What did you say about me?"

"Nothin'." He turns away. Since he's backed down, I return to my girlfriend but I haven't even sat down beside her when he starts pointing at me again. Now my anger is overwhelming and there's only one answer for it. I walk straight back, tap him on the shoulder again, and as he turns I nail him across the face with a punch. I don't stop there; I pummel him with a twenty-shot combination across the face. Lefts and rights. Hooks, jabs, and uppercuts. Everything I can throw at him. He's still on his feet but completely rattled. I want a scrap to get out even more aggression, so I stand back to give him a chance to hit me. But he just puts up his hands as if to say no. The bouncer runs over and I raise my fists to him. Same thing. He puts his hands up as if to say, "No, thank you very much." I turn around and everyone in the bar is looking at me with their mouths open. I can hear police sirens, so I leave as quickly as I can, running straight back to the hostel.

What was I so angry about? The fat Aussie didn't really want to fight. He was just breaking my balls. He thought that telling me he was "from Queensland" might scare me away, as if Queensland folk were tough and I should already know that. I had just heard they were known for shagging sheep, not fighting. He definitely wasn't expecting to be attacked by an

Irishman half his size. When him and his mates saw how crazy I was, willing to take them all on by myself, they knew enough to realize that backing down and calling the cops was the better option. *This lad must not be the full shilling, so let's leave him be...* On my part, it had been a furious overreaction, which wasn't unusual for me at the time. I believed that if someone disrespected me, I needed to put them down no matter what.

That was my brain on drugs and alcohol, a combustible combination that fueled my anger and self-destructive rage.

SAN FRANCISCO, 2010.

This was my brain without drugs and alcohol:

I'm newly sober, trying to get through the steps. I'm told I need to go to meetings every day. The first couple were enjoyable, so this sounds kind of exciting. There are hundreds of different meetings around the city and I'm keen to go exploring, because I think they will all be cool. I find one on the meeting list in my neighborhood called "Ass in a Bag." That sounds right up my alley. I go to try it out one Thursday night, and it's full of these goths and gutter punks, homeless runaways who cause trouble around the Haight District. All the other meetings I've tried have been friendly, but not this one. The fun I'm having exploring my neighborhood meetings is about to come to an abrupt end. The secretary of the meeting asks me to read something. I'm kind of nervous, still self-conscious, but I agree and start reading. These fuckers start laughing. I'm the only Irish guy there, and I feel like they are making fun of my accent. I listen to them sniggering and feel that old familiar rush of anger. All I want to do is punch each and every one of them in the face.

But I don't. Because there are too many of them.

I wasn't completely naïve about the process of getting sober. It's not like I thought I'd suddenly become Gandhi, but—well, yes, I suppose I did—I thought I'd be exactly as calm as Gandhi! But driving home from Ass in a Bag I just couldn't tamp down my rage. Hands on the steering wheel in a death grip, all I could think was, *Fuck these pricks. Assholes making fun of me. Fuck this shit. I'm never coming back to these meetings again.*

Making fun of me... There it was again. I was so uncomfortable I didn't know what to do with myself, but I needed to do something. *Drink! That has always been my go-to when I feel like this. That would make me feel better.* The Hockey Haven was on the way home, and I decided I was going to stop in for a drink or two or ten. My sponsor, Dave, had been working with me since I first started going to meetings, and I decided to call him and let him know, thanks for trying, but I was done. Dave actually answered the phone, and I told him about the meeting and what I planned. He listened to the whole thing and asked me, "Richie, you didn't like drinking in every bar you ever went to, did you?" It depended on how badly I wanted a drink. If I wanted it badly enough, I didn't care if it was the Ritz-Carlton or the nearest gutter. But, in truth, I did prefer the grimier spots. If I had the choice.

"What? No, of course not."

"Well, you're not going to like every single meeting either. That's why you have to find the ones you like and keep going to those. Don't drink tonight. See if you still feel the same tomorrow."

Even though his analogy was a little soft, it made sense. I could drive by the Hockey Haven without stopping that night and see how I felt tomorrow. The next day, I had no interest in diving into a dive bar at all. If Dave hadn't answered his phone, though, I would have gone drinking for sure.

This idea of taking things one day at a time kept me from falling off the wagon, but it didn't address the underlying issues I was wrestling with. Or, more accurately, avoiding wrestling with. Lust, infidelity, dishonesty, violence—all these things that had me under their control before I was sober weren't just disappearing. They had been operating on autopilot for so many years, and I didn't really even know they existed until I began to look at them with my seventh step. If a horse thief gets sober, he's still a horse thief. I needed to work on these character defects with my higher power, by taking actions contrary to my usual bad reactions, before they would diminish.

Getting sober is an overwhelming and confusing time. All your defects, and the defense mechanisms you've developed to ignore them, come to the surface, and it's difficult to know what's what. Without booze or drugs to calm my reactions, these defects of character seemed uncontrollable.

The main guide to getting through the twelve steps to sobriety is the sponsor, someone who has completed the program and can show the new member how to navigate the difficult day-to-day journey. Bernard had wanted to be my sponsor from the start, but as much as I liked and admired him, I was afraid to choose him. He was Irish, and I didn't want an Irish guy for the job. I knew I would have to tell my sponsor all my embarrassing shit, and I worried Bernard would pass it along to the other Irish guys if I started drinking again or he started drinking again. I told him it would be better if I went with Dave, an American guy, because I didn't know Dave. It could be like a conflict of interest to go with Bernard. So, at the very start, Dave became my sponsor.

After Dave and I sealed the deal, I was determined to do whatever he asked. I called him every day, and we would also meet up and read the sobriety book about the program together. He always seemed busy. One night he said he had to work but we could meet up at the job. It was in a vacant apartment that had been occupied by a crystal meth addict who was now in jail. We got to this empty meth house, and Dave sat me in a chair in the middle of the room. He handed me the book and told me to start reading a particular chapter. I started reading to myself as he left the room and changed all the locks around the place. He came back when I was finished and said, "Okay, you're finished that step now."

As nice as it would have been to have actually completed the step that easily, I sensed something was wrong. I didn't know jack shit about getting sober, but this didn't seem like the way it was supposed to be done. Just a gut feeling. But one of my character defects is that I'm a paranoid, untrusting, and suspicious person. You would be too if you went through the shit I went through, being set up by the cops or betrayed by people close to you. So that day in the meth house with Dave I was struggling with what was true and what was my defect. *Is Dave not a good sponsor? Or am I just blaming others? Something just doesn't seem right about him. Should I have gone with Bernard? He's the one who brought me in to meetings in the first place. But Dave did talk me out of drinking after Ass in a Bag. Maybe Bernard would have too, though...*

Still unsure of myself, I called Bernard and explained what was going on with Dave. "I don't know, maybe it's me, but would you consider sponsoring me instead?"

Bernard joked with me at first, saying, "If I was sponsoring you, I could put you in your truck at the beach, and have you read the book while I go out for a surf!" He had this Santa Claus type laugh, a "Ho ho ho," kinda thing. Then he got serious. He said he wouldn't agree to sponsor me right off the bat, and insisted we meet before committing to each other. When we got together, he looked me right in the eye and asked me, "Are you willing to do whatever it takes to be sober?" That gave me a moment of fear. Whatever it takes? I mean, I wouldn't kill anyone—that was part of the reason I wanted to get sober. Or was he asking for a bribe to help me? Was he coming on to me? Was he making fun of me? Ahhh, there it was again. But I stopped myself. I started thinking about the here and now and not all the what-ifs, and I started to have some flashes of understanding. I knew that Bernard was my friend. I knew he just wanted to help me, and it came into focus how paranoid I was being. There was something in my way, something keeping me from being sober, and I was going to make sure I let this Irish block of a man help me. I looked Bernard right back in the eye and said, "Yeah. I am." He said, "Good. Alright. I'll be your sponsor."

(Turns out I had been right about Dave. Later, he came up to me and apologized, saying he had been high the whole time we were working together! Being right about my feeling of paranoia was satisfying, but it didn't seem like a healthy, spiritual way to think. Either way, high or not, Dave had stopped me from drinking that one time after Ass in a Bag, so I will always be grateful to him for that. Poor Dave tried to commit suicide by cop not long after, but luckily, they just shot him with the bean bag gun.)

Later, working with Bernard and struggling with Step Seven, I found myself confused again. What was I doing wrong? Was I not humble enough?

How was I going to rid myself of these defects? I knew that I wanted that answer as much as I ever wanted any drink. Dave had done his best to help me, and now Bernard was doing whatever he could. I felt supported, but still had a deep feeling of being adrift. That feeling was dragging me down with a steady, almost physical pull. I had to try and get my shit together. I was as scared as I had ever been about my future, until a cranky Irishman named Steven who really pissed me off one night showed me the path.

One of the first things both Dave and Bernard told me was that I would have to "get a commitment." A commitment is basically a job at a particular meeting—cleaning up, making coffee, passing the basket, or the like. The idea is to make sure you show up every week. One night it was announced that a commitment was available at my Monday meeting, so I put my hand up and volunteered without even knowing what the job was. They gave me the commitment and I was the new "greeter" for this meeting. I had to come a half hour early, stand at the door, and welcome people as they arrived. If I knew the commitment was for greeter I would have never volunteered because I didn't feel like talking to strangers or any of that kind of shit. I wanted to hide out in the back of the room and not talk to anybody, just try to recover in peace. But I had just volunteered to be a smiling face at the door. "Hey, how are you? Welcome to the meeting." That kind of shit. I really hated it because I was still shy and feeling bad.

After a while, I got into greeting a little bit more. I loved leaning up against the doorframe, smoking cigarettes, doing it really casually. One night, I was there doing my commitment as usual, chatting with people as they came in, when Steven came over. He was an older Irish dude, and he started giving me shit about how I was doing the job. In his Northern Irish accent he said, "Why don't ya stand up straight there? Fuckin' put out that cigarette. This isn't a very good representation of this meeting." I was so shocked by what he said that I didn't respond in the moment. It felt like a personal attack. I went into the meeting all pissed off, thinking, *This fucking prick, who does he think he is, giving me shit?* There it was—anger, rage, fury, call it whatever you like. It was churning deep inside me. I could feel my heart racing. My adrenaline was surging. It was like an old friend who came back to "paint the town" with me, just like the good old days. But I knew that this could destroy me. Why was I so quick to anger? Why did every slight pierce me to the core? I could not figure out why. (In hindsight, I can finally see it—*I was sensitive. Holy fuck. The sensitive gangster.* How lame is that? That's why I reacted with fury every time something bothered me.)

When I got home, I called Bernard and said, "Fuck this shit. Fuck this prick. I'm not going to these meetings anymore. This is bullshit." It had really hurt my feelings. I was so fragile at the time. Bernard listened to my rant. "I came here early to this meeting to do my fucking commitment as best I can and he's giving me shit about how I'm doing it. Fuck him. I'm quitting. I'm not going to this fucking meeting anymore. I quit."

"Hold on a second," Bernard said, "you don't fuckin' do that. That's your commitment. You agreed to do it."

"Yeah, but he gave me shit!" I remember that sounded weak even to me. I tried to build it up, said this guy was trying to derail my sobriety, or he was just an asshole and needed to be taught a lesson. He was not going to get away with making me feel...that way....

Bernard had no interest in my protests. "This is how we handle things when we're sober: If you have a problem with a man you fuckin' tell him what the problem is. You don't run away. Especially when ya have a commitment." Fuck sake. I asked him what he wanted me to do. "Call up that man and tell him you're annoyed about it." Annoyed about it!? I was furious. Bernard must not understand. Then he said that if I didn't call Steven and tell him how I felt then maybe he couldn't be my sponsor because I didn't mean it when I told him I would do anything to be sober.

I regretted opening my mouth. Now I had to call Steven. I definitely didn't want to call up this man who "annoyed" me, but Bernard had me. He knew that I wanted to be sober, and he knew what I needed to do.

I was really nervous, but I went outside to make the call. Smoked a few cigarettes and rang Steven. He answered the phone and said, "Hey, Richie, how's it going?"

"Steven. I've a fuckin' problem. You gave me shit on Monday night when I was out doing my commitment. You told me that I was a bad representation of the meeting because I was smoking cigarettes and leaning against the wall. That fuckin' pissed me off." I couldn't believe the words were coming out of my mouth. There was silence.

Then the funniest thing happened. He actually listened to what I said and responded, "You know what, you're right. I shouldn't have done that. I shouldn't have criticized ya. I'm sorry about that. Are we cool?" I said yes. We are. We're cool.

I hung up, a bit rocked. What just happened? All my anger evaporated. And I felt different. I started thinking about other things that had sent me into a rage and they simply didn't have a hold on me the way they once did. This sobriety was a weird business. If I was in a bar and someone had said to me what I had just said to Steven, I would have punched them in the face, not apologized and admitted I was wrong.

Ass in a Bag dickheads don't disappear just because you're sober. Neither do louts from Queensland or shitty bosses or other drivers who don't handle themselves on the road exactly as you'd like. Being sober doesn't make anger disappear either. But I was now realizing that my tools for conflict resolution could include more than "Fuck you!" or a punch in the face.

I began to see how important humility was at this step. There were so many things I had to admit I had no control over, including my anger, but one thing I could control was how I dealt with them. My reaction to unpleasant situations was the part I had to, and could, change.

If I hadn't beat the lugs off that guy in Australia I would have felt like a pussy, like I was a coward who let him get the better of me. Now, I realized that conflict and confrontation didn't need a winner and a loser, because no matter the outcome, my old style of dealing with anger hurt me as much as it might have hurt the person on the receiving end of my temper. This was no path to happiness. Having to be "right" was only my ego talking.

I began trying, on a regular basis, to ask my higher power to remove my defects of character and help me reach some sort of ego balance or humility. The defects still rear their ugly heads now and again, but I'm getting vast improvements, not perfection. I find myself better able to deal with my anger, to handle tough situations without flying off the handle. I'm not as sensitive as I was either. No needing to get upset when I'm criticized and no needing to prove something by battering someone either. It's not always easy, but, then again, it's not about comfort, it's about progress—not just towards living a sober life, but a happy life as well.

I went back to doing my commitment as greeter and Steven never gave me shit about it again. But I did find myself standing up straighter when I was doing it. And I tried not to smoke too many cigarettes either.

STEP EIGHT

ANOTHER SHIT LIST?!

—◆◆—

MAKE A LIST
OF PEOPLE YOU'VE HARMED

—◆◆—

STEP NINE

AND I HAVE TO DO SOMETHING ABOUT IT?!

———◆———

MAKE AMENDS TO THOSE PEOPLE
UNLESS DOING SO WILL BRING THEM OR
OTHERS HARM

———◆———

*(IF YOU ARE A CAREFUL READER YOU MIGHT HAVE
NOTICED THAT THIS CHAPTER HAS TWO STEPS.
THAT'S NOT BECAUSE THEY ARE SMALL STEPS
BUT BECAUSE THEY ARE SO LINKED TOGETHER
YOU KINDA GOTTA TAKE THEM IN ONE BITE.)*

IF YOU DRINK AND DO drugs for as many years as I did, you're going to find yourself in some pretty fucked-up places. Some shouldn't come as any big surprise: in police stations with some explaining to do; waking up in an apartment I don't recognize with a woman I don't remember; once I even woke up in an Andronico's supermarket not knowing how I got there...

But I never thought I would find myself, drunk or sober, standing outside a seminary, nervously trying to build up the courage to go inside. I wasn't there to take my vows and join the priesthood, but the reason I was there was equally unbelievable.

I was there to make amends.

Ever since my first meeting at the Irish Center, where I stood up and said, "I'm Richie and I'm an alcoholic and a drug addict," there was one step I was dreading more than any other, although it was really two steps:

—Step Eight was to make a list of all the people I had ever
   fucked over (they word that one differently but that's what
   it pretty much comes down to).

That list was going to be long.

—Step Nine was to make amends to them.

Seriously? *All* of them?

Step Four, when I had to make my shit list of all the people, places, and things I held grudges against, was hard enough, but I knew this one was going to be tougher. If you have a grudge against someone, you can keep it to yourself, but making amends to someone involves actually manning up, contacting them, and going over it with them—a far more daunting prospect. Even though many of my grudges had been issues of my own doing, some hadn't been, or the blame could at least be spread around. That was not the case with these steps. Everything on this list was going to be about me hurting someone, most times someone close to me who I truly cared about. Really consider this: You have to sit there and think about how miserable you made the people closest to you—put yourself in their shoes and feel their pain. Then you acknowledge what you have done to their face and try to make it right. It's so much easier to just pretend nothing happened, or that you don't care. Facing the people I wronged felt worse than any punching, stabbing, burning, or biting I ever got.

The previous steps had helped me to recognize my defects, and to (hopefully) have them removed. This allowed me to look back on my misdeeds with a clarity that was surprising and frightening. The recognition of these things was tough enough, but to know I had to deal with the people I had hurt was terrifying.

Another troubling fact was that I hadn't gotten caught for a lot of what I'd done, so a bunch of people didn't even know I was the one who'd fucked them over. Many of my actions were illegal, and I sure as hell didn't want to go to jail for things I had already gotten away with. I mean, there are limits to what you will do to be sober, and maximum security prison was farther than I was willing to go.

I went straight to Bernard. "Aw, fuck, man," I told him, "most of the bad shit I've done I haven't been punished for. If I get arrested for half of it, I'll be in jail for the rest of my life."

"Don't worry," he said. "We didn't get ya sober to send ya to jail."

Thank God.

The first two people on my list were easy: my mother and my wife. They were easy because they were the most obvious, but I also knew they would be the toughest to make amends to because of how much I'd hurt them.

My mother had gone through a lot, even though I had been able to keep most of my misdeeds hidden from her. There were times when I was severely coming down off ecstasy and would pretend I was hungover from drinking. My mother wouldn't know the difference. She had even found ecstasy pills one time. I think it fell out of my pants or something and she asked me what they were. I told her they were vitamins. Vitamins with Mitsubishi symbols on them.

But there were times when it was impossible to hide the fact that her son was a fuck-up. She had to bail me out when I got caught making fake IDs in high school, and I had no choice but to call her when I got busted for dealing. When she answered the phone, I told her, "Mam, I'm at the police station. I've been arrested. For dealing drugs."

She thought it was a practical joke. "Stop it," she said. "That's not funny."

I told her I was serious, but she refused to believe it, even laughing. That made it more difficult. I turned to the police superintendent and told him, "She doesn't believe me." He gravely took the phone and assured her that it wasn't a joke and she had to come and bail me out.

Up until that point she thought I was a good kid, apart from the usual dumb misbehavior boys got into. Nothing to lose sleep over. My arrest was a complete shock to her. Nobody from my family had ever been arrested before, let alone in trouble for something this serious. She never had any idea whatsoever that I was involved in taking drugs, never mind dealing them. I've never felt more ashamed than when I made that call, then had to watch my mother walk into the police station, the disbelief and confusion still on her face. Plus, the embarrassment of everyone from the area knowing what her son had done. I wasn't sure there would be any way to make amends for all I'd put her through.

I told Bernard my mother was the first person on my list, but she was over five thousand miles away in Ireland, and I didn't have the money or the time off work to go there and make my amends. He suggested I write her a letter. That sounded good to me. I had been dreading these face-to-face encounters and a letter sounded much easier. It wasn't. Putting into words all the ways I felt I had wronged her was painful and draining, but I did it and sent it off, worried about how she would receive it.

When my mother got the letter, she called me up and thanked me, told me how touched she was by it. She said she was glad I wasn't making her worry anymore.

I hung up the phone, pleased, but also a bit confused. Even though I dreaded interacting with people I had wronged, I hoped they would forgive me. My mom clearly did. But what I felt afterwards was happiness that my mom felt better. The amends I had made created healing for her, and that started changing me. The idea that I needed to be less selfish, and to look outward instead of inward, made sense to me, but up until that phone call it was all a bit theoretical. Knowing I had given my mom some peace of mind felt so much better than the relief that she forgave me. I wasn't the Grinch with a ten-times-bigger heart, but I felt a little better about myself, or at least hated myself a bit less. The recovery journey that had led me to this point became clear in a way it hadn't before. A light at the end of the tunnel that had just been a flicker since the moment I decided to get sober started to get a little bigger, a little brighter.

I only wished the next person on my list wasn't my wife. There would be no letter writing this time. This would be a face-to-face encounter, and I couldn't imagine how I could apologize for all I had put her through.

I was also worried because before Bernard sent me off to make amends to her, he told me some very important information. He said that if you are making amends to someone, you can't repeat the same behavior towards them. You can't cheat on your wife a bunch of times, make amends, and then go and cheat on her again. I tried to explain that I used to be Catholic(ish) and the whole confession/absolution routine was pretty sweet, but Bernard flatly said it didn't work like that in the program. It means changing your behavior forever and not repeating it. Otherwise the amends are bullshit.

I had stopped cheating as soon as I got sober. In my heart, I knew that if I started cheating again, I would end up drinking again, too. The guilt would get to me so much that I would need to. The thing about being sober is that if you start to do shady things, it brings you closer to a drink. If you aren't misbehaving, you're more likely to stay sober. But I still dreaded making amends to my wife because I had apologized so much for my behavior already in the past and then repeated the same shit.

Bernard told me there was no point in telling her about everything I had done. She had ideas about what had happened, I'm sure, but listing them out to her wasn't going to help the marriage recover. He recommended making amends to her in a general way.

I was planning on sitting down to talk to her but couldn't seem to find the right time. I kept looking for the right moment, but it never seemed to come. She always seemed like she was in a bad mood. If anything, there appeared to be more stress in our marriage now that I was getting sober. I know it sounds crazy, but I was feeling like she maybe didn't want me to clean myself up. Not that blatant, but it started changing the dynamic of our relationship in ways that I think she felt threatened by. I was no longer a helpless child in need of mothering. And to be very blunt, the woman you marry when you are strung out and stoned out of your mind might not be the same one you would marry sober. And vice versa, I am sure.

We were always an odd fit. There was that big age gap between us. She was a techie that worked in Silicon Valley, and I was an Irish troublemaker. She was quiet and reserved, and I was loud and obnoxious. But she was nice and smart, and we were both DJs. Of course, who wasn't a DJ in San Francisco back then? Oh, and she was hot. We just fell in with each other. Then she got pregnant and wanted to get married, and it seemed the right thing to do. We didn't know each other that well, and our understanding of one another was definitely not clear enough for this level of commitment.

So, I called Bernard at the end of the week to see if we could meet up again and plan more amends. He said he was too busy to meet me. This annoyed me, and I told him, "Fuck sake. Do you want me to drink again?!" He asked if I had done the two we already talked about. I told him I did one of them, the letter to my mother.

"Did you make amends to your wife?"

"No. Not yet."

"Why not?"

I told him I couldn't find the right moment.

"You're in the same fuckin' house! How can ya not find the right moment for it?! Now go and make fuckin' amends to your wife first before we do more."

I sighed. He was right. I was making up these excuses in my head. I had been avoiding doing it. So, I waited until the next night when the kids were in bed and told my wife I wanted to talk to her. She looked really worried, like I was going to tell her something terrible. But I just told her I was sorry about how I behaved when I was drinking and using. She hugged me and was relieved. Of all the "sorrys" I had given her, this one was different, and she could sense it. It didn't solve all of our past issues or the emerging new ones, but I was grateful that she was able to feel my sincerity.

Then I went back to my list, where I had written down my mother and wife as Numbers One and Two. I stared at the blank spot next to Number Three for a long time. It all seemed so overwhelming. How in the world was I going to be able to write down every single person I ever sold drugs to, let alone find them to make my amends? That was a lot of people. Hundreds. Thousands really, if you count the people I sold drugs to who then sold them on to others. I would never even know most of the people. It seemed physically impossible. Some people were dead too. How do you make amends to someone who is dead? Finally, I just wrote, "All the people I've sold drugs to."

I called up Bernard and said we needed to talk. It was funny—before I met him each time, I would try to work out in my head what I thought he would say. I would guess and see if I was right. A lot of the time, my guesses would be totally wrong. Bernard always seemed to surprise me. Part of the reason why I couldn't guess his response this time was that there are different kinds of amends you can make. Direct Amends are the type I made with my ma, where you confront the person you wronged and take responsibility for your actions. Another is Living Amends, where you make a genuine change to the way you live your life, showing others that you have stopped the sort of behavior that led to you hurting people. My amends to my wife were a combination of Direct and Living Amends. I was about to find out about the third type, Indirect Amends, where you find ways to repair damage that can't be undone.

Bernard and I met, and I told him about this long list of people I needed to make amends to for dealing drugs to them.

"What do you mean?"

"I have to make amends to all these people," I said. "I gave them the tools to destroy themselves."

He looked at me with the serious eyes he usually had. "Fuck sake," he said, "if you couldn't get your drugs from your regular dealer, where would ya get them?"

I said I would have found another dealer.

"A course," he said. "Sure they'd fuckin' do the same if they didn't get them off you!" I knew he was right. Drug addicts are tenacious in a way that is almost unbelievable. Look at me. I moved to a whole new country for better drugs. Bernard then said, "It's not like ya weren't takin' them yourself. You were fuckin' doin' them too!"

"So...what do I do to make amends?"

"Don't fuckin' sell drugs again! And help as many people to get off them as ya can."

While that was a relief, there were no easy amends. I dreaded having to do all of them. Even long-distance phone calls. I was so nervous, I would get in my truck, take my cigarettes out, and smoke five of them in a row. The funny thing was, sometimes I would call up somebody to make amends and they wouldn't know what the fuck I was talking about. It might be something I felt bad about for years, and they didn't even remember.

A particular one I remember well was calling a girl I lived with in Australia. She was a lovely person, but I had ridiculed her one day. I felt really bad in my heart about it because I had embarrassed her. It was cruel and I shouldn't have done it. So I rang her up to say I was sorry about how I'd behaved, and she had no idea what I was talking about. Not the foggiest. It was only me who'd felt bad about it. We had a little bit of a catch-up, and then I said goodbye. I smoked five more cigarettes right after. It was such a relief.

One of the main ideas in making amends is to not cause others more harm. Once I realized the girl from Australia didn't remember the hurtful thing I had said, I made sure to not go into detail about it. This concept actually became much more obvious in my next amends.

I had been dreading making amends to Travis, especially since he definitely didn't know how I had fucked him over. I met him near the end of my first year in college, when I started off heavy into ecstasy. To help pay for it, I had started dealing it. I was selling at one of those giant house parties with a hundred people and a DJ when I met Travis.

Travis was one of these older people, maybe thirty-something at the time. Kind of a dosser. A slacker. He didn't have any job that I knew of; I think he just sold hash. He came from Cork—Skibbereen, to be exact—and was a little bit of a hippie who wore glasses. Definitely not a tough guy at all. He may have even lived with me at one point. (The fact that I can't remember whether or not someone lived with me just shows the state of mind I was in from all of the drugs I was taking. Sometimes it's a bit blurry.)

Anyway, Travis said he had some cocaine—and would I like to buy any? I thought, *Why not? Coke sounds impressive. It might be better than ecstasy.* So, I bought my first gram off him. In hindsight it was probably some of the shittiest coke I've ever tried, but it still gave me a taste for more. It had probably been cut down a hell of a lot with mixing agents. It wasn't strong at all, but there was enough strength in it for me to identify it as something I wanted to do again.

I introduced Travis to Tommo, and Travis started buying hash from him.

(A quick explanation about the mechanics of selling drugs: Tommo liked to be a wholesaler, which meant he would sell large quantities of drugs to a few people—street dealers—who would in turn sell to their customers.

This way, Tommo wouldn't have to interact with a lot of people, which made the risk of getting busted smaller. He only needed four or five customers—maybe one person takes a couple of hundred pills, another might take a kilo of hash—to make a nice profit. But because he was selling larger quantities, he ran the risk of a longer jail sentence if he was caught. Like in any business, it's all about weighing risk versus reward. On the other hand, the street dealers interact with hundreds of people, increasing their odds of selling to a snitch, but with the smaller amount of drugs they were peddling, they faced less jail time.)

Now—and here's where all the trouble with Travis started—druggies are not renowned for managing their money well, so they often don't have the cash to buy drugs. So wholesalers and street dealers alike get their product "on tick" or on credit. A bunch of criminals borrowing money with no paper trail—what could go wrong?

Back to Travis. He wanted hash but didn't have the money to pay for it. Since Tommo had what passed for "good credit" with his supplier, he got the hash on tick for Travis, and Travis in turn got it on tick from Tommo. Travis agreed to pay Tommo later, as did Tommo to his supplier—a wonderful example of the efficiencies of gangster capitalism! The problem was that Travis took the hash on credit but had no intention of paying for it. He just went about selling the hash for himself and I'm sure smoking a lot of it too.

When Tommo tried to get his money, Travis just made a fool of him. He stopped answering his phone. He wasn't a tough guy, telling Tommo to fuck off; he just avoided him. This went on for a month or two.

On top of this drama with Travis, Tommo had other problems in Dublin city. His sleazeball cokehead roommate, Mick, had worked up massive debts with some other Dublin gang. Mick skipped town and went back to England. Tommo went to meet the gangsters in question and tell them what happened with Mick. They didn't take the news well and pulled a gun on him and tried to kill him.

I asked Tommo, "What kind of gun was it?"

He said, "Mush, I didn't stop to look at it! They were firing shots at me in the fuckin' street. I just ran for me life!"

Tommo was also starting to get pressured by his supplier, "Smiling Pat" from Navan. (This isn't "Pat the Rat" from our gang. That's another Pat. If you're Irish you'll know a lot of Pats or Patricks.) Smiling Pat might have been just a teenager, but he was the scariest sixteen-year-old I've ever met—a young Irish Scarface. What he lacked in age he made up for in pure insanity. He had his own arms dump of machine guns and hand grenades that he bought from some terrorists and would sell to any willing buyer. He was threatening Tommo on the phone with power tools, running drills and saws and the like, telling Tommo that this was what he was going to get if he didn't pay his tab.

This is where my need to make amends to Travis started.

The only way for Tommo to get off the hook with Smiling Pat was to get the money from Travis. But Travis clearly had no intention of paying. (Maybe some of the people Travis sold to on tick hadn't paid *him*— who knows? Everyone in the drug world is running on the same hamster wheel.) To get the money to pay off his supplier, Tommo proposed the idea of kidnapping Travis. And he wanted my help.

At this point, I was also on the hamster wheel. Tommo would give me a hundred or a couple hundred ecstasy pills on credit. I would end up taking half of them or giving them away, or giving them to people on credit who didn't pay for them. I would always end up owing him more money each time, and he would just keep giving me more and more pills. The bill was growing. He was throwing good money after bad and I could never seem to get my shit together. By the time of the Travis incident, I owed Tommo a lot of money. I think it must have been over a grand. I just know it was way more than I could pay back. I was sinking in my own quicksand.

Now, Tommo told me that if I helped him and his crew kidnap Travis, to get ransom money to pay the debt he owed, Tommo would write off my debt to him. This was my lifeline, but I was hesitant. I said I didn't want to help if they were going to kill Travis. He didn't deserve to die. Tommo assured me that they wouldn't kill him. "His family are rich," he said. "They can pay what he owes. We'll just scare them and get them to pay the money he owes if they want to see him alive again. Plus, they'll pay the kidnapper's fee." (Each of Tommo's crew were to be paid five hundred pounds for their part in it.)

We agreed 100 percent that they weren't going to hurt Travis. All I had to do was keep an eye out for him, and whenever I saw him, stay on him and call Tommo to let him know. Him and the boys would come down from Dublin and pick Travis up. They would then take him to a safe house in Dublin that they had ready.

One night soon after, I was down in a bar called The Roost and spotted Travis. The Roost was the happening spot in Maynooth, with two levels and a back bar, a DJ playing the latest hits, always jam-packed full of people—the type of place where it takes twenty minutes to get served at the bar. Not exactly the best place for a snatch and grab, but I texted Tommo to let him know I had eyes on Travis. He called me and warned me to stay on him until they got there. I watched him for a while until he left, and I followed him outside and up to another bar called Caulfields. Caulfields was almost the exact opposite of The Roost. It was a quiet old man's pub up the street, sleepy and comfortable. They had great Guinness (because they took their time pouring so it settled properly while The Roost fired them out like a factory because a huge crowd was always waiting for more). It was the perfect place for a conversation or a comedown.

Or a kidnapping, because there were no bouncers or crowds about. The bar was maybe half full.

I sat in a dark corner and texted Tommo to let him know where we were. The crew arrived at the pub soon after—Tommo, Anto, Martin, and Scotty. (He's known as Scotty because he's from Scotland. Scotty was in his thirties by this stage. Legend has it that during his first arrest in Ireland he didn't have any ID with him and told the cops he was sixteen. In actuality he was in his mid-twenties. They sent him to a juvenile detention center for a few years. Scotty was massive, so he must have been the boss of that place.)

Tommo and his crew marched into the bar and looked around. Travis was sitting at a table. When he saw the men who came for him, he went white as a ghost. He knew the jig was up. Standing in front of his table, Tommo said, "Mush, come on, you're coming with us. Up to Dublin." There was no kicking or screaming, no fighting, no arguing. He just stood up, took it like a man, and walked out with them. You could see he was scared, though. He didn't know if he would be coming back alive.

Before he walked out with them, I had been feeling good about the whole thing. He had welched on a debt and was getting what he deserved. I was helping my friend out of a bad spot and wiping my own slate clean in the process. But when they were walking out, the guilt hit me. Travis had saved my life before. The first time I tried to kill myself, he had hid my pills from me. And here I was being his Judas. Setting him up to save my own skin and get out of my debt. If I'd said no, they probably would have done that to me.

Regardless, it all hit me as they were walking out the door together. At that moment, I felt like a piece of shit for what I had done. I guess part of me knew what Travis did was wrong, but the guilt wracked me anyway. I never believed that they would kill him, though. If it had been just some random person who hadn't saved my life before, I don't think I would have felt the guilt. But it was personal to me.

Tommo told me later what happened. They took Travis up to Dublin in the car, not saying a word. That must have been an uncomfortable ride. Then they took him to the so-called "safe house," which was actually just Tommo's house because he didn't have a real safe house. When they got him into the house, they basically tried to scare him.

"Mush! Ya have to call your parents and get your family to pay this money ya owe."

At first, Travis was pretending his parents didn't have any money. In the middle of this, Tommo's gay brother comes into the room with a tray full of tea for everyone. "Mush! Get the fuck outta here, will ya, you're ruining the mood!"

It sounded quite comical.

So back they went to trying to scare Travis. Apparently, what really got to him was this: Tommo went into the kitchen and came out with trash bags. Travis was told, "Look, Mush, this is your last chance. You get the money or you're going in the fuckin' bin bags if ya don't call them."

Travis agreed to call his parents, tell them he was in danger, and that they had to pay the money that was owed. I think it was six or seven thousand in total. This included the kidnappers' fees and my fee on top of the drug debt. The parents were told to bring the money up to Dublin and meet at this deserted parking lot. If they brought the money, Travis would be let go unharmed.

I'm not too sure how soon it was, whether it was that day or the next, but Travis's parents came to Dublin and Tommo went to collect the money. He pretended he was just working for the kidnappers as a bag man. He had an Arab scarf tied around his face to conceal his identity. Travis's mother arrived with the money and Tommo pretended to be someone else. She pleaded with him, "Please don't hurt Travis!" but Tommo just said, "Mush, I don't know anything about it. I'm just here to pick up the money." He got the money and they let Travis go. That was the end of it.

Travis never mentioned it to me when I saw him after that, and I was convinced he had no idea I had anything to do with it. But now, years later, the guilt hit me hard all over again.

I looked at my list where it said "Travis's kidnapping" and racked my brain trying to figure out how to handle this one. Saying "sorry" didn't seem nearly enough for what I'd put him through. I felt like I needed to do something much bigger to make amends to him. *Hmmm,* I thought. *What's the opposite of a kidnapping?* Then I hit on it. A vacation! That's the exact opposite of a kidnapping!

I met Bernard, gave him the lowdown, and told him my idea for amends. "I'm thinking a vacation, maybe to the South of Spain." I was making more money by now, so affording that was possible.

Bernard smiled at the thought of sunny Spain but then asked me, "Does that man know you were involved in the kidnappin'?"

"No..."

"Well why the fuck would ya tell him?!!"

I told him that I felt bad about it.

He said, "Ya fuckin' eejit. Ya don't say anything to him about it."

"So I shouldn't send him on a vacation?"

"No. Just don't fuckin' kidnap him or anyone else again! That's probably the worst experience of the man's life. There's no point bringing it up to him now."

His point hit home. Never make the wronged person's life worse just to make yourself feel better.

I was way off with my estimations for other amends as well. Good thing I ran them off Bernard or I might have really fucked things up. In fact, Bernard might have literally saved my life with the next person on my list.

When I was working construction, I stole some tools from one of my employers, someone who I thought had been unfair with me. This guy was next up on my list. This one particular contractor would have been quite dangerous, actually. He was capable of putting me in the intensive care unit. Knowing his temper, if I came up to him and said, "Sorry, I stole your nail gun," he would likely beat the fucking head off me right there and then. He wouldn't be grateful to get the stuff back; he would be more outraged that I had taken it.

Fortunately, Bernard knew this man well. I was prepared to walk up to the guy and take what was coming, but Bernard warned me against it. He said, "Are you fuckin' well in the head?! If you went up and told that man he would beat the shit out of ya there on the street." I told him I knew that but didn't know what else to do. He told me, "Whatever them tools are worth, just donate that money to charity." I definitely felt a relief right then. I had the money. So I donated about a thousand dollars to charity and kept my head attached to my shoulders for another day.

Having money in my pocket that I once used to spend on drugs and alcohol made the amends easier, and in some cases, very satisfying, like in the case of Tommo.

Even though I had gotten square with Tommo on Travis's kidnapping, I ended up going back in debt to him—a debt I had never paid. It was probably only a few hundred bucks, but it had been a long time and I felt bad about it. So when I went back to visit Ireland, I stopped by his house and left a Christmas envelope there with cash in it—the money I owed him plus interest. He didn't find it for a month or two. When he did, he rang me up and thanked me for it, saying it had arrived at a time when he really needed it. So that made me feel good, knowing I had actually helped someone.

I was getting into a groove with my amends. Make a call. Write a letter. Do a good deed. I was like a sober Santy Claus. Still, there was one thing I knew I still had to make amends for, but I had no idea where to begin. It wasn't the worst thing I had done, but it definitely ended up being the most complicated one to try and put right. It was all about a painting.

I can't recount all the specifics about the caper because it will incriminate innocent people that don't deserve to be incriminated. Remember, the point is not to fuck up other people's lives so you can make your amends. It happened around recession time—2008 or 2009, a couple of years before I got sober. Things were tough for a drug-addicted carpenter. Work was scarce and I had burned a bridge or two in town with my behavior. As a result of this, I found myself working for a moving company to make ends meet.

Stealing stuff is easy when you're a mover. There's always confusion about what is being brought and where it's packed, so if you were so inclined it was pretty easy to get away with. There was an old guy I worked with—well, actually, he couldn't have been that old, but moving is a hard life and he may have been forty but looked well into his sixties. Anyway, he told me, "Always take your own tip. If they don't tip you at the end of the job, just keep something. But if they do, just give it back and pretend you forgot it was left in the truck." This procedure was known as the mover's insurance policy.

One day, I got a pretty sweet gig. It was a week-long move job for this billionaire. He had a massive art collection. A lot of good stuff, with no inventory, I might add. I had a feeling he might stiff us at the end of the week, so I started "shopping" for a painting I could use for my mover's insurance policy. I wasn't much into the modern stuff, but a nice prairie picture from the 1800s caught my eye.

The colorful landscape reminded me a bit of home, and it was only about thirty-six inches by forty-eight inches, a manageable size. Lo and behold the client did stiff us, so I left with a nice old painting behind the seat of my truck. I'm no art expert, but the sales sticker on the back told me it was purchased from a gallery in one of Silicon Valley's most expensive towns, and what little research I dared to do told me it was worth over $100,000—definitely more than a 1 percent tip.

Once I stole it, I mailed it back to Ireland straight away. All of the packing and shipping materials were at the ready from the moving truck. I wrapped it really well so it wouldn't get damaged and sent it by regular mail. No point in using a courier because there was more chance of it being checked. Now if the cops came looking for it, there would be no evidence. It was gone.

I can't say who took care of it in Ireland because, as I mentioned, I don't want to incriminate them. But somebody took care of it for me back in the old country. My plan was to wait for however many years or decades as was needed until it was safe to sell, and have a nice nest egg or a retirement plan. It turned out that the painting was never missed, though. At least the cops never came near me if it was, or I never heard anything about it on the news. So I had totally gotten away with it.

One time, I went back to Ireland for a visit before I got sober. I was curious to see how my painting was doing in safekeeping. Hopefully my nest egg was in good shape. I called over to see my buddy who had it, but I couldn't track him down. This was worrying. Had he sold it and moved to Spain? Next, I called to his mother's house. She said he would be back soon and let me in to wait. I had a nervous cup of tea with her in their living room. Finally, my friend showed up. As I walked into the kitchen to talk to him, I noticed something. Bejaysus! There it was hanging on the wall of his mother's kitchen, hiding in plain sight for all to see. People walking by it all the time and nobody knew it was worth a fortune. "What the hell is going on?" I asked my buddy. He said that his mother dug it out of storage and liked it so she hung it up. He didn't want to tell her it was stolen and figured that it might be safer in plain sight.

You know what? He was right.

Now I was sober and I couldn't keep that painting. So, I called Ireland and had it mailed back to me in San Francisco. As soon as it arrived, I knew I had to get rid of it quickly. The adrenaline of stealing it came back to me, and I started to feel uneasy. I was on the straight and narrow now, and this painting reminded me of my past. I'd learned that any unfinished business, any guilt that wasn't dealt with, could lead to a relapse. I opened the package to make sure there was no damage to the painting, wiped it down in case there were any fingerprints on it, then wrapped it back up.

I wasn't too sure how to proceed with the situation, because this was considered grand theft. There was a risk that if I walked up to the place it was stolen from and handed it over saying, "Sorry about this, I stole it," and they took it the wrong way, I could be talking to the police—they'd press charges and I'd go to jail.

Of course, I asked Bernard what to do with it. He didn't know. He asked his sponsor. His sponsor didn't know either. We went up the line and nobody could figure out how to do this.

The good thing about the meetings is that you can find people from many different backgrounds to talk to. If you have a problem, there is a pretty good chance there is someone working the program who is an expert on it. Our ranks are a bit over-represented in the fields of law and law enforcement, so we put out the word on the dry drunk hotline. We asked cops; we asked lawyers. I even asked this old IRA terrorist friend of mine, John. He devised this scheme that was fairly complicated. It involved wrapping up the painting, stashing it somewhere, and then making an anonymous call from a phone booth to have it picked up. Tell them it's in a certain place and it needs to be picked up. Like a military operation. That was John's harebrained scheme. We figured it was too risky in case someone else found the painting or something went wrong, and ended up not doing that one.

We eventually did come up with a plan though...

That's how I found myself sitting in front of a seminary, trying to get the balls to go inside. The drive down to the seminary had been worse than any of those times I was hammered and feared being pulled over for a DUI. Now, I was clean and sober, but that wouldn't matter much to a cop who pulled me over and wondered about that big box in my truck. "Oh, how interesting. This was reported stolen three years ago..."

I made it to the seminary without incident, then sat outside a long time, smoking cigarette after cigarette. I finally built up enough nerve to go inside. A woman behind the desk greeted me, and I told her I wanted to make a confession—was there a priest available? I'm sure I looked quite grave, and she immediately called someone for me. It felt like I sat there waiting for hours, with all the saints and martyrs staring at me.

I specifically remember St. Sebastian full of arrows giving me a look like, "See what you did to me?" My anxiety was building and I started sweating. Memories of my Catholic childhood and the confessional flooded over me, and I remembered the old ritual and the traditional prayer. Then a priest walked in, and I followed him into the chapel. I can't really remember what he looked like because my adrenaline was so high. I know he didn't remind me of any of the dickhead priests from school. First of all, I'm pretty sure he was really young and he had no air of arrogance about him. But there was a bigger difference—this priest seemed like he cared about me. He seemed... holy. There was a calm warmth to him that I can still feel even if I can't picture him.

The priest sat next to me and asked me what was going on. "Look, Father, I stole a painting before I got sober and it's worth a lot of money. I need to give it back or I won't stay sober. I need to get this off my conscience and I don't want to go to jail for it. I was wondering if you could give it back for me?" And then, in what felt as quick as a lightning bolt, he said, "Of course." It was like he answered before I finished my sentence. Like he knew why I was there before I even entered the sanctuary.

No surprise. No questions. Just acceptance.

We walked outside together and went to my truck. The painting didn't weigh much, but once I handed it to him, I felt an enormous weight lifted from me. Driving away from that place, I felt like a million bucks, even though I had just given away the most valuable thing I had ever owned. It was such a relief because I knew it wasn't mine and I didn't have to worry about it anymore.

It crossed my mind that the priest might keep it. But I knew that wasn't the case. I just knew it in my heart. Before this day I had this grudge against the whole Catholic Church because of some assholes I had met in Catholic school, but now this was completely gone. There were a lot of good priests out there, and I had been focusing on the few bad ones I knew from school or had read about in the newspapers.

That's the way it was with most of the amends. I felt changed. Even though there were some people who wanted nothing to do with me—and I couldn't blame them—I still felt like these amends were making me whole. All the bad things I had done in the past had been traveling with me all those years, dragging me down like a backpack loaded with bricks. At long last, though, I didn't have to worry about them anymore. There was nobody from my past who I had to avoid, couldn't look in the eye, or had to worry about bumping into.

I could stop looking over my shoulder, and finally start looking forward.

THE PERSON YOU MARRY WHEN YOU ARE TOTALLY FUCKED UP MIGHT NOT BE WHO YOU WOULD MARRY WHEN YOU ARE SOBER... AND OTHER REALIZATIONS

CONTINUE PERSONAL INVENTORY AND RIGHT NEW WRONGS

THE IRISH BAR WHERE I met my wife was called "Anú," which is the Gaelic word for "forever." "Forever" doesn't really translate into the language of alcoholics and drug addicts. The only future we care about is the next drink or drug. Even recovered substance abusers are taught to take things one day at a time. So, when I swore in my wedding vows to stay with my wife forever, I had no understanding of the commitment I was making.

After making my amends, I was able to move on in a healthy way with pretty much everyone in my life. Most of them, though, were in my past, or only occasionally present. It wasn't that difficult to start on Step Ten, which was to continue taking a personal inventory and righting new wrongs. I had learned to rely on my higher power and had developed the skills to deal with my anger and to resolve conflicts in a positive way. My relationships grew stronger. At least it felt that way at first. As I continued down that road to sobriety, though, it became very clear that one relationship was going in the other direction—the one with my wife.

After all the work I had put in to get sober and making amends to my wife, I assumed a happy ending was inevitable. It wasn't. I was not the same man she had married. But I was better, right? I certainly couldn't be worse.

During my years of drinking and doing drugs as a married man, I would have never been a candidate to win "husband of the year." And that was when I even bothered to come home. I was usually out partying somewhere, and, more times than I care to admit, fucking around with other women. I not only cheated on my wife with steady girlfriends, I cheated on my girlfriends with hookers. It was almost like a twisted math equation that ended up **Richie Stephens = Lying Cheating Asshole**. I'm not sure you could label me a sex addict, but I often found myself in some extraordinary sexual situations that I think most sober people would never encounter, and definitely wouldn't indulge in. Especially when I was on the coke.

One day I was drinking and doing coke at the Hockey Haven when a fine young woman came in. She was a little bit older than me and had a mischievous look about her I found intriguing. We started chatting and drinking together. I discovered she was a teacher, which turned me on even more (I know a lot of people fantasize about their teachers, but I had mostly priests as teachers, so this was a new and exciting fantasy for me). She was very flirtatious, so I asked her if she wanted to do some coke. We went outside, and I led her around the corner to a school. I thought it would be fun to do blow with a teacher outside a school, and it was!

We ended up making out and getting horny. I think she would have fucked me right there, but it was broad daylight and I worried about getting caught. So we got into my truck and started fucking...in broad daylight! People were walking by and I just couldn't relax, so I asked her if we could go back to her place. She said no, her place was a mess, then asked if we could go back to my place. I said no, because my wife was at home.

"You think she'd be up for a threesome?"

Holy shit, this woman was game for anything. As tempting as it was, reason took over and I told her my wife would kill the two of us if we came back to the house.

We drove down to Golden Gate Park. At this point it was starting to get dark. I parked the truck, and we got out and walked to a wooded area. We lay down on the grass. There was nobody around, so we started fucking right there. The usual high-powered coke sex. Then, all of a sudden, I heard something. It was a rustling sound. I looked up and there was a homeless man right in front of us. He was watching us and jerking off. Just standing over us, beating off. Literally three feet away. I shouted at him, "HEY! HEY! FUCK OFF!"

He totally ignored me, kept on whacking off. If someone ignores you when you catch them masturbating and you tell them to stop but they just keep going, then it's obvious there's no point arguing with them; that person is not of sound mind. We definitely couldn't finish the job, but he was intent on finishing himself.

We got up and left him there still pulling his wire.

Next, we hit this cheap motel by the beach. Crazy sex all night. Lots of cocaine. My new favorite teacher said, "Let's have an affair! Let's get the same room every time we have sex!"

I said, "Fair enough, sounds good to me."

We started meeting up every week, but after a few coked-up fuck sessions she wanted me to leave my wife. Even though I was constantly cheating on her, I still felt committed to our vows in my own fucked-up way, so I told Teach that was not going to happen. She did not find my twisted commitment to my wife honorable, charming, or sexy anymore and showed me the road.

Another time, my wife and I went to a wedding of a friend of hers in San Jose. Weddings are supposed to be romantic, right? Bridesmaids and groomsmen hook up for one-night stands, married couples go home and have wild sex... At this particular blessed event, I drank so much I could barely stand. The only answer to that was to do some coke. I called my dealer, Ronald, to see if he could deliver a bag to the wedding for me. He couldn't, but said that he would drop one off when I got back to San Francisco. We left the wedding early and it was maybe ten or eleven o'clock at night when we arrived back home. I told my wife to drop me off at a bar—Ireland's 32 on Geary Street—because I wanted to go and drink more on my own. She dropped me off without complaint. I didn't bother to think about it at the time, but I guess she wasn't looking over at the drunken mess next to her and thinking romantic thoughts, either.

Into the bar I went, dressed like Scarface in my black suit and red tie. The plan was to party like Scarface too. I got the bag of coke as soon as I arrived and then bumped into a guy named Noel, a funny little ginger man from Mayo in the west of Ireland. We ended up drinking a lot, and then he invited me back to his place to do more coke.

We started doing some lines in his living room. Maybe a little of the romance at the wedding rubbed off on me after all because pretty soon we decided to get hookers. "Love is in the air," as the song goes. We went on Craigslist, found a couple of girls, and invited them over. I had never ordered a hooker off Craigslist before because I usually just went to massage parlors. But seeing as we were at Noel's place, we could just have them come to us.

A bit later, these two young ladies in their early twenties came over. They were pretty cool, and we chatted and did coke with them. Noel didn't have any money, so I agreed to loan him the money for his. I think they were two or three hundred apiece. I had a couple of hundred on me in cash, which I gave to them. They said I could go to the bank machine later and pay them the rest. You could tell they were pretty new to the game because they would never have agreed to payment later if they weren't. We did some more coke. They had brought meth with them, so we did some of that as well.

Noel took his girl into his bedroom, which left me alone with my girl in the living room. We got jiggy on the couch. Afterwards we did a little more coke and smoked some cigarettes. Noel and his lady came back out of the bedroom, and I said I'd go up to the ATM to get the rest of the money for the girls. I asked Noel where the nearest bank machine was, and he said it was twenty blocks away.

"Twenty blocks? Can I borrow your car?"

"No way. You're too drunk."

I assured him I was fine to drive, but the answer was still no. I saw a bicycle in his kitchen. "Can I borrow your bike? I could be there and back in ten minutes."

Noel just shook his head. "No, I'm tired, I'm going to bed."

Then he walked into his bedroom and shut the door. Left me there with the two girls. *Motherfucker. He wants me to pay for his girl and won't even let me borrow his bike to go to the ATM. That's a forty-block round trip that's gonna take an hour to walk. What a prick.*

I said, "Okay, girls. I'll be back. I'm just going up to the ATM."

I glumly left the apartment, lit up a cigarette, and started walking up Clement Street towards the ATM. When I reached about fifteen blocks up, I had an epiphany. *Fuck it. I just won't go back. Let that little prick pay them himself. I already gave them a couple of hundred bucks and coke for everyone. Noel expects me to walk twenty blocks to the ATM and twenty blocks back to pay his bill and he won't even let me borrow his push bike. Uh-uh. I'm just walking home.* So I breezed past the ATM and continued heading back home. Another twenty blocks to go. Smoking cigarettes, whistling away to myself, and hoping those girls have a pimp to deal with Noel.

My phone started ringing. It was the hookers. They asked if I was coming back. I said, "Yeah. I'm just on my way to the ATM."

They said, "You better come back, because if you don't, we're gonna take your friend's laptop!"

I assured them I would. Then I turned off the phone and home I went. I climbed into bed next to my wife and was hit with a pang of guilt. But it had nothing to do with the woman I married, the mother of my children. I actually felt bad about not paying the girls the rest of the money.

When I look back at those times, it is with tremendous shame. I wasn't proud of the kind of husband I had become, I just didn't have the tools to do anything about it, other than booze and drugs to numb my feelings and get out of my own head. My wife didn't take it all lying down. We would argue or she'd give me the silent scorn. My reaction was always the same: *Fuck her, I'm going to the Hockey Haven, to drink, do drugs, and not come home for a few days!* Then I'd lie about it all. Especially the drugs.

My wife didn't mind me drinking, but I was not allowed to do coke. The constant challenge for me was trying to hide the symptoms before I got home—the fast heartbeat, bug eyes, runny nose. There's a couple of ways of doing this. You can drink a load of beer, but that takes hours. You can smoke weed, but that stinks. I used to stop at the pharmacy on the way home and get a bottle of codeine cough medicine. Downing the little bottle would pretty much level me out. Probably did serious damage to my liver, though.

Communication was never good between us. One night, when I was near my all-time low, she walked in and found me loading my gun, clearly intent on killing myself. Before I even realized what was happening, she grabbed the gun and ran from the apartment, fucking up my plan. This was probably a good time to discuss that there might be some problems in our relationship, but when she returned neither one of us mentioned it. A wife stops her husband from killing himself and neither one ever speaks of it again. I doubt we would have done too well on *The Newlywed Game*.

My wife did try to straighten me out when I came back from Australia. My girlfriend and I had broken up while we were there, and when I returned I moved back in with my family and tried to give it another shot. My wife agreed, but on the condition that I go see a shrink. I did. She was a nice lady. At my first session I had to fill out what seemed like a phone book full of paperwork. All kinds of shit, from my height and weight to my family medical history.

There was a section that talked about my alcohol and drug consumption. I didn't want to seem like too much of a fiend, so I was conservative with the volume of drinking and drugs I admitted doing. I said I only drank around six pints and snorted a mere half bag of cocaine on a night out. That seemed like gentlemanly amounts to me. In reality, I'd go out and drink ten pints on average and the guts of an eight ball of coke. When the shrink and I began talking, she told me straight out that she thought I was an alcoholic and drug addict and should go to twelve-step meetings.

I thought that was preposterous. I was sure I had some other kind of mental illness or depression. "Let's talk about my childhood," I told her. That kept her busy, and fair play to her she never broke down and prescribed the drugs that I was hinting at but did not need.

Bottom line, nothing changed my behavior until I started doing the steps and didn't want to cheat anymore.

All long-term relationships evolve. Our marriage did as well. The moment my wife walked into that bar, I was taken with her. My roommate Andy was a bartender there and he had invited her, probably hoping to seal the deal himself, but nothing had happened between them so she was still fair game. He was too busy pulling pints behind the bar anyway. You snooze, you lose. I was coked up as usual. I was first attracted to her because she was hot, but it was her maturity and chill nature that really hooked me. Most of the girls I dated had been my own age and fond of the old Persian Rugs (drugs) like I was. She didn't do drugs but didn't seem to mind that I did. I liked how she was quiet and easygoing. I'm fairly laid-back in relationships, so a bossy woman was the last thing I wanted. We got on like a house on fire at the beginning. It seemed effortless.

Once we had kids, things began to change. My wife expected me to go from drunken party boy to mature, responsible family man overnight. I never got the memo. The added pressure just made my reliance on drink and drugs worse. Resentments piled up on both sides, and our relationship slid into a parody of a marriage. For me, though, it worked. I could call myself a dutiful husband and father because I didn't abandon my wife and kids, but I could also continue to party and fuck around with other women. At some level, it must have worked for her as well, because she never left me. That is the most confusing thing to me to this day; she figured out how to deal with being with the most fucked-up version of me. I don't really know how, but she found a groove that made sense to her and arranged her life to accommodate it.

When I got sober, I tried to get all of my shit together in life, including the marriage. The road was rocky from the start. When I was partying, I was barely home. Then, when I started the twelve steps, I was out again, because Bernard told me I should go to a meeting every night. Even though I wasn't at a bar or a whorehouse, she was still angry I wasn't around. This was the first change in our relationship. She thought I should just be able to stay home and not drink. She did not like me going outside for help.

While I was drinking, I let my wife make most of the decisions in terms of what we would do or not do. Where we would shop or spend Thanksgiving. Shit like that. I didn't care because I was medicated. But now, sober me started to have opinions. She wasn't used to that, and she didn't like it. She was used to being in charge. Also, she had seen mostly dumbass behavior from me for the previous five years, and still thought I was a fool.

But I wasn't a kid anymore, and I wasn't that same cokehead she had married. I had changed, and felt different about myself than she did. This was the root of the conflict.

My old friend, Anger, started buddying up to me again, whispering in my ear. *What the fuck's her problem? I'm trying to get better and she's just making it harder. Maybe she doesn't want me to get my shit together. Maybe she wants to keep calling all the shots.*

I felt my wife looked at me like a piece of shit someone had brought into the house on the bottom of their shoe. She complained that I got dirty doing construction work. She complained that I didn't have much money. She complained that I smoked cigarettes (even though I never did it in the house and always changed clothes to do it!). My old reaction to this kind of stuff, the three Ds—Drink, Drugs, Disappear—wasn't an option anymore, so I would fall back on the new tools I had learned for dealing with things that upset me: Go to a meeting. Call another alcoholic. Pray. This kind of shit, instead of using it as an excuse to get wasted. That was the key to Step Ten. I was examining my behavior, using the tools I had learned, and tried to modify my reactions to avoid the inevitable conflict. These new solutions took some getting used to, but they were working. Only for me, though.

I don't mean to portray the trouble in our new dynamic as all her fault. I had unrealistic expectations of how I should be treated once I got sober. Me and the missus now had zero spark in the romance department. That had been on the decline for a few years but had reached an all-time low now. The way I saw it, she should be throwing herself at me now that I had got my shit together, but she was more likely to be throwing things *at* me. It was like I could do nothing right, and things were getting worse between us when logically things should have been getting better. I'll admit, when I saw some of the attractive women at the meetings, I was tempted by them. My drunk logic was still lurking in the background telling me that might actually be a good fix for everyone. But I was trying to be a good sober person and that didn't include cheating. That was old behavior.

Next, I received a tempting offer. I got invited to the Playboy Mansion! Well, really Alfredo got invited and he was going to bring me along. He was my old Filipino buddy from the Hockey Haven. Alfredo was a roadie for Carlos Santana and I used to sell coke to the musicians in the band. He had all sorts of Hollywood friends and now he was inviting me to come along for the party of a lifetime in Hugh Heffner's crib. I ran it by the guys in my group and they obviously didn't recommend it. I knew they were right. I had to let it go. Booze and nude models would be too much temptation for a newly sober fella who was trying to be a good and faithful husband. In the end, Alfredo ended up bringing some chick who really embarrassed him because she kept cursing in front of the other guests.

I insisted we go to marriage counseling to try and fix things. We went every week together, but my wife didn't make any effort. She just behaved negatively and didn't want to change anything. In the course of this counseling, I realized that I wasn't in my right mind when I had agreed to get married and start a family. It was like waking up from a dream and seeing you have a wife and two kids now. The weekly sessions helped me a lot more than they helped "us." After a few months, I realized that it was a waste of time because me and the counselor were the only ones trying.

My resentment towards her was growing every day. Thank God I had Bernard to talk to or I don't know what I would have done. He pointed out something that really helped me—that my wife didn't have all the tools I did to deal with the stress in our marriage. She had suddenly found herself married to a completely different man, creating a brand-new dynamic, and she didn't have a sponsor or group to talk to or help her—or even more important—a higher power like I did. She was figuring it all out on her own. This realization that it wasn't all about me helped me avoid the old trap of going into full victim mode like I had in the past.

By doing a personal inventory, I could clearly see my part in all of it. Over the last few years I hadn't been a good husband or dad, and that wouldn't be easy for her to forget. Just because I was behaving better and had stayed sober for a few months, it didn't fix everything that happened before. It didn't erase all the bad memories. I was able to have some compassion and patience with my wife. On top of that, I was supposed to be doing a living amends for how I had behaved in the past. Part of that was going to be dealing with these problems and not giving up. My job was to keep doing my best in recovery and trying to become a better person.

Just as drinking and doing drugs affects the people around the user, getting sober has repercussions as well. The life I had created for myself as an alcoholic and addict wasn't the same life I would choose as a sober person. And it was also true for the people close to me. Old Richie, who never turned down an invitation to party, was attractive to some people, and the defects in my character that led to substance abuse were appealing for some reason to certain people too. The new Richie wasn't the guy some people wanted to spend time with. Other people, like my wife, were so burnt out from dealing with me as an addict that they didn't have the energy to work on a whole new relationship with me. She had gone through her own transformation to figure out how to live with me and wasn't up for a new twist. And maybe she never believed it would really work.

My wife and I spent several more years trying to save our marriage, but we eventually got divorced. It was the most difficult experience I faced as a sober person. I had a tough time making peace with the fact that sobriety, and all the tools I had learned getting there, weren't enough to solve every problem I faced. Sometimes things just don't work out. Some people aren't meant for each other. And for some people, my old ways were easier to live with than my new ways. My ex-wife was a combination of all these things. She had seen the worst of me, and she simply could not forget that. The damage done was too great and could not be repaired. When I eventually realized that, and was able to drop any expectations that my ex would suddenly view me as a good person, I could move on with my life, wherever it was going. Even though my relationship with her had ended, I could still try to be a good dad to my kids.

I was resolved that my old ways were behind me for good, and that a new life lay ahead. I had no idea what that new life was about to throw at me.

STEP ELEVEN

LUCKY BREAK

PRAY AND MEDITATE

WHEN I WAS LITTLE, THE local priest, known as "Father Blather," told us the story of Job. Job was a fella who did nothing wrong, worshipped God faithfully, then got the living shit kicked out of everything he cared about, just because of some stupid bet God had with Satan. I remember thinking that God wasn't very nice to pull that shit on poor Job. A few decades later, when I was new to sobriety, I suddenly became reminded of this story.

I was far from the sinless Job, but I was really trying to be a better person. Getting sober made me realize I had been wasting my life, and now I had the chance for a new start, a reset that could change my path and bring me a happy, productive one. This meant doubling down on the new spiritual practices I had learned, and building my life back up. The urge I had to get started was as strong as any jones I ever had for drugs. I needed to *go go go*, to make up for lost time and catch up with the normal people who hadn't burned their lives to the ground with drugs and alcohol.

I began to get my house in order. One thing that had been hanging over me for years was money that I owed the IRS. A few years earlier, I worked a construction job for an American guy named Ben. I think my friend Crazy PJ got me in with the company. He was called "Crazy PJ" because he was a crazy good fighter. We knew another PJ known as "PJ The Machine" because he was a really fast worker. If you're Irish, you know a lot of PJs. After the project was over, Ben told me there was no more work, paid me, and we said our goodbyes. Oddly enough, I heard from PJ that the rest of the crew then started on a new site without me. I knew I was by far the best worker, but I was the only one let go. I was mad as hell, and, as any good addict would do, I blamed someone else—Ben—for the whole thing.

At the end of the year, I received a 1099 in the mail from Ben's company. He had paid me as an independent contractor, so it was my responsibility to pay the taxes on the income myself. When the envelope arrived and I saw what it was, I didn't open it. I just took a big black marker, put an X across my name and address, then wrote on the envelope, "Return to sender. And tell sender to go fuck himself." Once I was sober and able to look back at the incident with clarity, I realized I was always angry on that job because I felt like I was working with a lot of dipshits, and at the time I had little tolerance or patience for dipshits, partly because they were clearly having trouble appreciating my obvious brilliance. Being hungover or strung out all the time didn't make me the nicest person. Everyone was scared of me, understandably enough, and Ben clearly just got sick of my shit and figured I wasn't worth the trouble. I'm sure I was bad for team morale.

After I popped the notice into the mailbox, I forgot all about it. Unfortunately, the IRS didn't. I got several notices after that, warning me about penalties and possible jail time. I ignored all those too. Now, though, I wanted to make up for my past transgressions, so I contacted the IRS. Considering the fact that I'd come forward, I expected a bit of a pat on the back or at least some leniency, but neither were forthcoming. Clearly, the IRS had the same problem as the "dipshits" from the job. Now that I was sober, though, I decided to just go with the flow...as much as I could, considering the penalties were more than the taxes. But I paid it all and kept a smile on my face, if not completely in my heart, and it did feel good to set things right.

My credit was also a mess, because of an incident with Ferret ("Cavan Ferret," to be clear). He didn't have a green card when he first came to America, so I let him get a car in my name. The only condition I made was that he had to pay any traffic tickets he got. He didn't; they went to a collection agency and totally fucked my credit. I never confronted him about it like a normal person would; instead, I tried to fight him at a workmate's wedding up in Sonoma when I was drunk. He didn't even know why I had tried to headbutt him.

We didn't speak for years after that. Eventually, we bumped into each other at an AC/DC concert in Oakland and made peace (I recall it was while they were playing "Moneytalks" but that just seems too perfect to be true). I was on a roll. So now I went about contacting all the companies I owed money to and started to fix my credit. This was daunting, but like we say, "One day at a time," so I just kept my head down and started chipping away. It was like a video game to me. I had a big spreadsheet, and I would make payments until I could delete them from the sheet. After a little while, the whole thing was gone. Pow!

To really get my life in order, though, I knew I had to take a serious look at my career. Even back when I was drunk and using drugs, I could see that working as a mover was a dead-end job. A lot of friends were working construction, and I thought that could be a career with a future, so I reached out to my friend, Arthur, who brought me on to learn how to be a carpenter. At the time I didn't know jack shit about construction, didn't even know what a "two by four" was on my first day. That's how clueless I was. At the start they just had me cleaning up and shit like that, but the money was good *(More drugs! More booze!)* so I stuck with it.

Then I learned how to use the tools, and slowly I got better at it. Arthur gave me dog's abuse constantly. In his thick West Cork accent, he would call me a "tick (thick) cunt" at least twenty times a day. He would ridicule me every time I made a mistake, which was often, but it toughened me up. Working with him was like being in the Marines with a hard-driving drill sergeant. But he could also be hilarious. Every time I cut something wrong, he would say, "Hey, maybe you should stick to dealing drugs..." He definitely had my number, and one time told me, "You know what your problem is? You're smart in all the wrong ways, boy."

The work was hard, but I could see the possibility of making a lot of money in the future. Even though I was high most of the time, I was really good at my job. I started thinking about getting my contractor license so that I could start my own business—do my own jobs and be the boss. But it remained only a barstool fantasy; I committed my free time to more drinking and more drugs instead of studying to get my license.

Once I got sober, though, and with my past mistakes taken care of, I was ready to put in the time and effort to become a contractor. It was going to require experience, hard work, and a license, but I was up for it. Without partying to distract me, it was easy to find the time to pursue my license. I got the study books and took all the classes. To be a general contractor, you need to learn a bit about everything. I was a carpenter but had to learn about plumbing, electrical, landscaping…all sorts of shit. Plus, contractor laws. I worked really hard and took the test. I passed them all except one module (the law test, not surprisingly), which I had to repeat. Second time was the charm; I passed and received my license. I was still employed by someone else, but now I was free to go out on my own whenever I wanted. The pause button was lifted, and finally, I was catching up in the game of life.

Before starting meetings, the absolute longest I was able to stay dry on my own was three months. I had now beaten that record, and there was no sign of me relapsing at all. The cravings to get high went away, with the help of my daily praying and meditating. Three months became six months, then nine. I was on my way to becoming one year sober, which was mind-blowing because I previously didn't think this was possible. I had always thought I would be dead by this time.

The Bible tells us, "There was a man in the land of Uz, whose name was Job; and that man was perfect and upright, and one that feared God, and eschewed evil." I was still far from perfect and upright, but I had faith in my higher power and was eschewing my greatest evils: alcohol and drugs. I got up every morning, happy to be alive and looking forward to what the coming day held.

This was probably the same way Job felt, until it all went to shit.

Job's trials started when he caught the eye of Satan; mine began when I met Killian. Killian was an Irish property tycoon, like a diminutive Irish Donald Trump. He owned property all over and was well connected around San Francisco with politicians and government officials. Killian was definitely a grifter, and was notorious for graft and corruption—really crooked. One day, when I first started working construction for him, he called me up and asked if I wanted to be a building inspector. "We need one of our people in there," he told me. I had only just qualified for my contractor license though, and you needed to be in business for four years before you could take this position. That didn't seem to bother Killian, but when I hesitated, he must have found someone else better suited for this scheme because he never mentioned it to me again. Even though he could be a bit of a bully sometimes, I liked him and found his success to be inspirational.

Working for Killian, I'd go from job to job, usually with his number one guy, Gordon, another sober Irishman I'd known a while. Gordon ran jobs for Killian, who treated him like a son. A lot of times, Killian would take Gordon away from a construction site around noon to go to the Olympic Club and play golf. I would be left alone to continue the work with the crew and day laborers. At this point, I knew exactly what to do on a job without having to be told and could be left to work on my own without any problems.

One June day, we were doing a remodel on Hill Street in the Mission District. The house was held up by cribbing, stacks of posts, and we had to put some new support beams in an existing ceiling. Gordon and a Mexican guy called "Murphy" (that was his nickname because he spoke English with an Irish accent) were lifting up a beam to put in place. It was a big fucker, about the weight of a piano. We had a shitty, makeshift scaffold to stand on, made from "two by fours" and "two by twelves" just nailed together. Not the safest thing to be standing on. Five or six people were needed to lift the beam, not just the three of us. We tried to lift it up into place, but it wouldn't fit. We were really struggling. I shouted to Gordon that it wouldn't work, but he wouldn't accept that and tried to force it. It bounced back out of place, and he put up his hands to protect himself. Then the beam swung around and hit me on the shoulder, knocking me off the scaffold and down to the ground. It was about a four-foot drop, but I had been hit hard by the beam, fell backwards, and landed on my ass. Luckily, the beam fell down on the other side away from me.

I started shaking. Something was definitely wrong. The beam had hit me on the shoulder, but I felt pain in the bottom of my spine. It was really bad. I was kind of in shock, but I was able to stand up, and thought it wasn't too serious, that maybe I'd just pulled a muscle in my back. Gordon chopped an inch off the beam, and we put it up again. This time it fit properly. The day was pretty much over and it was time to go home. I didn't feel right but thought I would be fine. That evening, I was in a lot of pain, but I was pretty tough. I never thought about going to the doctor or anything. I just thought it was something minor.

The next day I went back to work even though I was still hurting. Walking around was difficult. I did light stuff for a while but had to stop because it was so painful. I thought maybe it was a trapped nerve and I should get a massage. I took off work early and went to see a physiotherapist we knew called Sidney. The massage was so painful I couldn't even let him finish it. I was literally screaming from the pain. It seemed obvious that I would have to take a couple of weeks off work because it was so bad.

That was a long two weeks. I was in pain, and had none of the usual distractions—the drugs and drink of the old days, or the work of my new sober days. But I didn't let it get me down. I did my usual shit, prayed to my higher power, went to meetings every day, and soldiered on.

After two weeks, my back hadn't gotten any better so I went to the doctor. He sent me for an X-ray but nothing showed up. That was a relief; I thought maybe I just needed more time. To be sure, though, the doctor sent me for an MRI, and that's when I discovered the truth: My back was broken. I had one broken disc and another herniated one. The doctor didn't phrase it this way, but his tone said, "Your back is really fucked up." Pain was radiating down the back of my left leg, and I had to go to the bathroom a lot.

Still, I didn't let my situation get me down. I had faith everything would be okay. There was no way the old higher power had helped me to get sober and put me on the right road to become a cripple. I figured this was just a setback and everything would work out right.

The doctor said some people were helped by cortisone injections in the spine, so I tried that. They were really painful and didn't help at all. Then the doctor suggested a "neurolytic block," which tries to kill the pain by burning the nerves in your back. Maybe this would be the solution. It wasn't.

I began to get frustrated. *I wonder if a drink, or some weed would make me feel better...maybe some Vicodin...* Ironically, before pot was legal, I once made up a back injury in order to get a marijuana card. The doctor gave me a prescription for OxyContin too, so I was well armed, even though I had no back problems at all. Oxy were great for coming down off coke, so for years I would take them on the way in the door from a night out. After an eight ball of coke ricocheting around in my skull, I would double drop two Oxies before bed, and within a half hour I would be out like a light. (I only wish I had discovered Oxy before spending all those years drinking codeine cough syrup to hide the coke symptoms.)

With my back broken, I really needed pain relief. I knew that a lot of other addicts and alcoholics fell off the wagon when they started taking painkillers, though, so instead I prayed and went to meetings, and occasionally took some ibuprofen if the agony became unbearable.

The possibility that I would have to live with this pain started to become a reality, and I was starting to question what was in store for me. I knew for sure I couldn't have got sober without the old higher power, but this didn't feel like it should be the plan for me. I didn't have much choice, though, but to see what was next. It wasn't easy, but I was committed to playing with the cards I had been dealt without descending into self-pity or blame, which would have unavoidably led to drinking and drugs. I wasn't exactly sure how I would be able to go back to work, but I planned my return.

Then, the doctor told me there was a danger my injury could lead to me becoming paralyzed. I made the doctor repeat that twice; I just couldn't believe it. That night, the prayers to my higher power took on a very different tone.

Are you fucking kidding me? I finally get my life in order and this is my reward?!

I needed surgery, something called a microdiscectomy. This involved them opening me up, shaving off one of my back bones, and reaching in to take out the broken piece. I agreed. What choice did I have? I was really scared, though. The doc said that there was even a tiny chance of death or paralysis from the surgery. The night before going under the knife I asked my higher power to help me through this. I think I may have even mentioned in my prayers that my higher power owed me one.

(A quick aside, just because the incident really freaked me out. They knocked me out for the surgery, and when I awoke in the recovery room I was wearing only the hospital gown and had a massive hard-on. That struck me as weird. I wondered if someone had been interfering with me as I slept. A nurse in the room noticed I was awake and came over. She asked if I was okay. I was fairly wide-eyed, trying to figure out why I had a boner. She asked, "Do you have a hard-on?" I said, "Yeah, you could say that." She told me, "That's normal." Thank God. So weird. Being turned on by life-threatening medical procedures would be a strange fetish to be into. The nurse left, off on her rounds, leaving me with a giant horn on me.)

The wife didn't even offer to pick me up from surgery. She was still mad about all of my old behavior. Instead, my buddy Will, a comedian I knew from meetings, picked me up and dropped me home.

The operation was a "success." They removed half of one disc, which eliminated the threat of potential paralysis. Plus, I was still alive! The doctor then told me that with one half disc missing, my career as a carpenter was over. I could no longer lift anything remotely heavy, or my disc would pop out and the pain would lay me up for a month.

I began to spiral. *I'm not going to make a full recovery?! Why me? I'm doing everything right! How could my higher power let this happen to me?* There it was again: self-pity, blaming others. Now, though, I could recognize the feelings coming and was able to stop them. But for how long?

Since my injury, I had been living off my savings. When I had first gone to the hospital, I didn't mention I was hurt on the job. I considered Killian to be a friend and didn't want to cause him trouble by ratting on him at the hospital. His workers' comp premiums would have gone through the roof, and he could have gotten into trouble for having an unsafe jobsite. Months had gone by, though, and he hadn't paid me anything. All of my savings were disappearing.

Gordon was telling me on a weekly basis that Killian would take care of me. "Don't worry. It's going to be fine. Killian is going to sort you out." Eventually, with nearly all of my money gone, and still unable to work, I had to do something. I rang up Killian and told him I was almost broke and that I never reported my injury happening on the job. I asked him what he was going to do to help me. He invited me to meet him for coffee the next day. I headed over to Noe Valley, and Killian was there waiting for me with Gordon beside him. I hadn't expected Gordon to be there too. Before I could sit down, Killian said, "You called me looking for money yesterday. I can't have you taking up space in my head." He was annoyed, an attitude I wasn't expecting.

"I got hurt working a job for you."

Before I could go on, Gordon piped up.

"Your back was already fucked. You didn't hurt your back on the job. It was already fucked." I couldn't believe what I was hearing. *This Judas motherfucker.* For months he had been telling me that Killian was going to help me out, and now he was lying to my face to support Killian, totally stabbing me in the back. Pun intended.

"I got hurt on jobs before and I never got paid anything," Killian said.

I could feel my fury building, but I kept my cool. "Killian, I've always worked hard for you. And I didn't tell anyone I got hurt on the job, to save you money. Now, I can't pay my rent."

"Richie, if I told my wife that you wanted me to give you money, she would say, 'He wants money, tell him to go get a fuckin' lawyer!'" This was more bullshit. His wife was a mail-order bride from Thailand who was thirty years younger than him. I told him I wasn't trying to scam anyone here; I really got hurt and was his employee when it happened. I didn't rat on him, and now he was turning his back on me.

Killian took a deep breath. "How much is your rent?"

"Twelve hundred a month."

Then, as if he was doing me the biggest favor in the world, he told me he could pay my rent this month and just not tell his wife about it. I couldn't believe what I was hearing. This motherfucker lived in a thirty-million-dollar house in Pacific Heights and he was offering to pay me *one* month's rent.

With that I lost my temper, said "Fuck you," got up from the table, and walked out. I knew he didn't want to help me, and I was so angry about Gordon betraying me that I just left. Leaving was the best option because I felt like smashing their two heads together.

That night, I prayed to my higher power as usual, but my heart wasn't in it. The focus just wasn't there. It seemed like the higher power wasn't going to help. I started to think that maybe this could be payback for all the bad things I had done in the past.

After my meeting with Killian, I gave up trying to get anything from him. I didn't know what else to do. Christmas came, and I had to borrow money from my buddy Alfredo to buy presents for my kids. Even during my years of drinking and doing drugs, I had never felt so lost. Or been so broke. I really had no idea what I was going to do with myself. My plan for the next forty years had been to work in construction, start my own company, get a big crew, and build shit around the city while making a fortune. That dream, which seemed so achievable, was now shattered.

I was broke. My back was broke. The future looked grim. The self-pity and blame game came knocking on my door again, and now, I let it in. *What the fuck? I thought everything was supposed to be good when you get sober. Why are you doing this to me, God? I thought we had a deal. I'd be good, do the right thing, and everything would be okay. What the fuck?!*

I knew one good way to make money—dealing drugs. The temptation to go back to a life of crime had never been so strong, but I knew that would also lead to drinking and doing drugs too. *So what? My life is ruined... I have no future anyway.*

When I had told my supplier, Ronald, I was done dealing drugs, he had left an offer available for the future. He said if I ever wanted to come back and work for him, the door would always be open. All I would have to do is answer his phone and drive around San Francisco doing deliveries of coke. Five hundred bucks a day. No questions asked. This now started to look like an option. I told myself, "If all the money runs out, then I'll call Ronald."

I shared honestly at meetings about how I was feeling. That's what I had been taught to do. One night, I told everyone, "When all my money runs out, I'm going to go back to dealing for my old gang." People gasped. When it was over, Pat Maguire came up to me. He looked me right in the eye and told me, "You're just keeping that one thing in your back pocket so you don't have to rely on your higher power." He was right. It had been my escape plan, should all else fail. He said, "If you rely on your higher power, you'll never have to do those things again." This proposition was scary—being willing to 100 percent trust my higher power and risk losing everything.

I realized, though, that the most important thing to me was not relapsing; I didn't want to let everyone down who had stood by me for close to a year. I kept going to meetings, but every time I was asked to share it was all, "Poor me, my back is fucked, I have no money, I don't know what to do..." That kind of shit, because that's how I was feeling. I wasn't being a good sport. The other folks in the meeting were supportive, telling me to be strong, to keep praying and meditating, and everything would work out. I didn't believe it, but I was so close to being one year sober that I was able to hang on. But it was getting tougher every day.

There was an old priest who used to be a regular at the meetings. The poor guy had a stroke and was now in a nursing home in Pacifica. He was so fucked up he wasn't able to get out to meetings, so a bunch of people started going down to visit the guy, taking meetings to him in the nursing home. Steven encouraged me to come along with them for a visit, and I grudgingly agreed to go. When I met the poor old guy, I realized he could barely speak. Half his body was paralyzed. When I saw this fella stuck in a hospital bed, I gained some humility. I realized that as bad as my situation was, there were people much worse off than me. I'm sure Steven knew when I saw this poor guy, I wouldn't feel so sorry for myself. Not that it put a huge dent in the amount of complaining I was doing. I knew I was annoying everyone but I just couldn't stop myself.

There was a guy in our group called Pat O'Hara. He was nice but kind of annoying too. Everyone kept away from him. He was coming down to visit the priest also, and nobody wanted him in their car, so I ended up having to bring him in my truck. The two annoying fuckers traveling together. I got stuck with Pat O'Hara for a half hour on the way down to Pacifica. We were chatting (i.e., I was complaining) while I was driving. Pat asked me what happened to me, and I told him the whole story. Up until this point, I figured that was the end of it. Tough luck. I had got fucked over by Killian.

"You should sue that guy," Pat said.

I immediately dismissed the idea, because Irish people don't really do that. At least they didn't when I was growing up. There was a general distrust of the law and government, so you took care of business personally. I told Pat this, but part of his annoying personality was that he couldn't let things go. He kept saying, "You should sue his ass. He's a piece of shit. He can't do that to you." By the end of the trip to Pacifica and back, Pat O'Hara had convinced me to sue Killian. Employers have a responsibility to their workers when they get hurt on their jobs, and Killian had totally ignored his duty to me.

That night, I thought about what Pat Maguire had said too, how I hadn't been "all in" with my higher power. He was right. I hadn't been willing to take whatever was coming to me. Going back to dealing never should have been an option, no matter what. I decided that I would never do that again— even if I ended up living on the streets.

I moved forward with suing Killian, thinking maybe I could get some of the money I had lost through no fault of my own, and get back on the path to a new future. I began to once again feel some hope.

The lawsuit against Killian took years to go through the courts. My lawyer was a deadbeat who ignored my calls and did little to win the case. Early on, I was so paranoid that I even thought there was an outside chance Killian could have me whacked. He didn't have the background I had, in terms of criminality, but whacking me would have been waaaaay cheaper than going to court. In the end, I think Killian got weary of paying his high-priced lawyers and offered a "just go and fuck off" settlement. He falsified backdated payroll for me and was able to pawn most of it off onto workers' comp. I got a fraction of the money I felt I was owed, ending up with less than a year's wages in compensation. That's all I got for a lifetime injury.

I know people who got injured at work, won two million dollars in compensation, and were fully fit after a couple of months. Good for them. I may not have ended up with the money I was hoping for, but still, I felt like a winner. I came out the other side, still sober.

That wasn't all. So many nights when I prayed, it was with anger or frustration or self-pity. *Why me? How could you do this to me?* Now, though, I was praying in a whole new way. More calmly. More earnestly, I guess. Having better acceptance when things didn't go my way. And the whole experience gave me something else, which has proven to be even more valuable: a renewed and redefined faith in my higher power. Throughout it all, I relied on the idea that God/my higher power had a plan. That working construction, breaking my back, being fucked over by Killian, then finding some answer by traveling with a really annoying Irishman was the path laid out for me, ending in a predetermined result.

After this, though, I realized that for me, turning myself over to a higher power did not mean I had to have faith that there was some preordained plan with a known endpoint where everything would be okay; all I had to do was leave the outcome up to the big fella. At one time this would have been impossible—the idea of blind faith was scary and difficult to follow for me, because I didn't know whether things would work out. Then, I realized my faith wasn't really blind at all. I was seeing actual evidence that this shit was working. Bernard, the meetings, my program, my higher power. All of it. I had faced everything thrown at me and had stayed sober.

The few bucks I was awarded after my accident did help me pay back all the money I owed (including Alfredo for the Christmas gifts), but by then my life had already moved on in another direction.

STEP TWELVE

PUT ME IN, COACH!

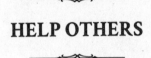

HELP OTHERS

THE IRISH ARE A LYRICAL, talkative people and have some great sayings and proverbs. I always liked Murphy's law: "Whatever can go wrong will go wrong." And one that I found all too relatable: "Whenever you see someone with a black eye, you say, 'There's a fella who was talking when he should've been listening.'"

As I looked at my life after my injury and was unable to work as a carpenter, I found myself repeating a line from an old song by Doris Day, who admittedly wasn't Irish, but that I first heard sung by my Irish mom: "Que Sera, Sera, whatever will be will be..." It was really just a catchier way of saying, "I will have faith my higher power will take care of me."

I had completed eleven of the twelve steps in my pursuit of sobriety. I had faced everything that was thrown at me, and with the help of faith, friends, and family—and my sponsors—I didn't relapse. Staying sober is not a paid occupation, though, and I had to find a new career and make money, but had no idea what I wanted to do with the rest of my life. That kind of uncertainty is not ideal for a person in recovery. I had to find something to do every day if I had any chance of avoiding a relapse, because another phrase my mother always said to me when I was a kid was "Idleness is the devil's workshop."

All I knew to do was keep going to meetings. They were my only source of stability, a lifeline in the sea I found myself floundering in. The only meeting I was ever tempted to miss was my Saturday morning one. It was a bitch, not because I was hungover from a wild Friday night, but because I had the coffee commitment, meaning I had to get up real early to get there before anyone else and make the coffee. When you go early, though, you always end up meeting people, chatting and making friends. One of these people was Wayne. He was a computer expert, and one of the original programmers for PayPal, but the booze had him living in his car when I met him. Even though the grog had got him down, you could tell by just talking to him that he was extremely intelligent, and gave you the feeling that if he could stay sober he could possibly create the next Google. He started telling me about how he was making good money designing websites and—bang!—it hit me. *I'll fucking make websites too.* That's something I could do with a broken back: just go to City College and learn this shit. So, from talking to Wayne, I found a new path; I would go back to school and learn how to make websites.

I enrolled at City College and started taking classes in web design, HTML, and editing. I enjoyed making sites and found it satisfying in ways that I did with construction—figuring out solutions to problems when things didn't look right, and a feeling of accomplishment walking away having built something. I wasn't fired up to get out of bed every morning and sit at a computer all day, but it was definitely something.

Around this time, Bernard told me I needed to start sponsoring other dudes who wanted to get sober. (Bernard was not particularly sexist for an Irishman of his years; he was just being realistic about who was going to get help from me.) This was the last step, Step Twelve, To Help Others.

"You can't keep it if you don't give it away," he told me. "Otherwise, you'll only end up relapsing." I was kind of dreading being a sponsor because I was at a low point; I still wasn't excited about the future, and I just felt myself getting pushed along towards it. I was waiting to see "whatever will be will be." How was I supposed to help anyone when my own new sober life was going down the tubes? It was hard to be a positive inspiration for someone else if you were feeling sorry for yourself. Bernard never understood the word "no," so I agreed, but I made no effort to sponsor anyone, and no one came looking to me for help. Who is going to ask a sad sack to sponsor them?

One day, sitting in a meeting, wondering if building websites was really what I could see myself doing for a living, my friend Lori turned around to talk to me. She was a nice, sweet person. "You should be a model," she said. Now I had used that line a few times in my day, but Lori knew I was married and we were definitely just friends. "Wait, are you serious?" I said. "I'm too old to be a model. And my nose has been broken too many times to make the grade." Lori said I had a "look," though, and insisted I consider it.

Another popular phrase in Ireland is, "God loves a tryer, but he hates a chancer," meaning, keep trying and you'll get ahead, but don't be dishonest about it. It's similar to the Gaelic football phrase, "Take your points and the goals will come." In other words, keep showing up for the small scores and the big ones will come on their own.

So, after kicking it around in my head a bit, I thought, *Fuck it. I'll give it a shot.* I was broke, and I knew models didn't have to carry heavy shit. And it didn't mean I had to give up on web design, so I figured why not? My commitment to web design was clearly weak though, because I decided to quit school, determining I could go online and teach myself anything else I needed to know after that one semester.

I had to get some headshots taken, and I found a few photographers who would take them for free—they got some practice, and I got the photos. These were hit and miss, with the big majority being misses. Then someone referred me to an Eastern European dude called Slava, who gave me a good deal to take some real, professional headshots.

At night, I would secretly go to my computer and email my headshots to various modeling agencies. I didn't tell my wife because she was always in a bad mood and made it clear she didn't think I would ever be successful at anything. If I told her I was trying to be a model, it would have just put more pressure on me to succeed, and when I failed, it would be that much more embarrassing. I also thought it could possibly jinx me. I am not sure where jinxes fit in with higher powers but I am a big believer in them.

I was in no hurry to tell the guys at my meetings either. Since my lawsuit with Killian, I had stopped hanging out with many of the Irish guys because a lot of them worked for him. They weren't saying much about how I had been treated because they were still reliant on him to make a living. Now I was hanging with the Narrowbacks, or Irish Americans. When I first heard the term, I asked Arthur, "What's a Narrowback?" He responded, "Ya know…like the pig." My knowledge of pigs was limited, but I got the idea. It was supposed to mean less than a pure breed. In response, some of the Narrowbacks called the Irish-Irish "donkeys." Some of the bogmen from Ireland walk with a funny gait or "gatch" as Arthur called it—humping around just like donkeys.

I was a donkey hanging with the Narrowbacks.

Most of those guys were super blue-collar—plumbers, firemen, cops, working for the sewer company, etc. I had a feeling they might think I was coming out of the closet if I told them I was becoming a model, so I kept it quiet at the start.

One of the agencies actually replied and wanted to sign me. I couldn't believe it. They were a shitty agency, but I was a total beginner, so even a shitty agency was good and I signed with them. I was so happy that I told my wife as soon as I walked in the door. She snarled at me, "So what, my cousin has an agent!" I guess at this point in our relationship my wife was not exactly encouraging me and hoping I would succeed.

The agency sent me out on a few casting calls, and I booked a few small jobs here and there. Nothing to change my life but enough for me to keep at it. Enough, also, that I felt I had to tell the guys at the meetings. Honesty was part of being sober, so I shared in one meeting and told them I had started modeling. I was prepared for the jokes, but instead everyone was really supportive. They didn't break my balls about it once. I guess they knew I was having a hard time losing my career as a carpenter and they were happy I found something new (and legal) to do.

I learned a little more about the industry and loaded some pics online to a site called Model Mayhem. A director who was casting a gangster film saw my picture and reached out to me. His name was Weston, and he told me he was making a super-low budget indie movie and he wanted me to be in it. "Think you could play a German gangster?" he asked. Even though I had never acted, I had never modeled or worked as a carpenter either—

until the first day on those jobs. Always a "tryer," bordering on "chancer." And, for some reason, I've always been able to do different accents. Like how musical people can tune a piano by ear, I'm like that with voices. As a carpenter, I always did accents on the job, taking the piss out of people I worked with.

"Sure, Weston, I could do that," I said. And just like that, I was an actor.

We shot my scene in a warehouse in San Ramon, California. My character had some information on the whereabouts of some stolen money, and two hitmen were going to interrogate me. I was tied to a chair, and Weston explained that the other actors were going to "beat" me to get me to talk.

"Any questions?" Weston asked.

"No," I replied. I knew exactly what to do. Because I had been in that situation before.

It was a Sunday night in 2001, back in the old country, in Maynooth. I was in the house I shared with two other ne'er-do-wells, and at around nine o' clock there was a knock on the door. I had already gone to bed, but I got up, in my underwear, to answer it. Sullivan stood on the front step with two other men I recognized, Scarecrow and Dan. Sullivan was a local bad guy, a psychopath who didn't go to college but liked to party with us, and we never had any problems with him. He respected us and we respected him. He was a lunatic, though. At one of our house parties, Sullivan found a cycling helmet, put it on, and started smashing empty bottles over his head, one after the other. Laughing like a madman, hammering these bottles off the helmet while it was on his head, and the rest of us looking on in amazement. Even while off my nut on pills, this looked crazy. He was a tough fighter too, really strong and brutal. I knew that he was involved in robbing a mail truck around this time. Scarecrow brought it up once, telling us how they went through the mail sacks, looting all the birthday cards. Sullivan promptly told him, "Shut up, will ya!" So Scarecrow zipped it right away. You didn't want to set Sullivan off.

I remember saying, "Hi..." when I saw them standing there, but that was all I could get out before Dan and Scarecrow shoved me into an armchair while Sullivan went barreling into the kitchen. I was puzzled, to say the least, especially when Sullivan came back holding a bread knife.

This all felt very wrong and very bad. "What's going on, Sullivan?" I said.

He didn't answer, just put the knife on my coffee table, near an empty shot glass my friend Lynda had bought for me as a gift from her holiday in Lanzarote. I hadn't even used it yet.

Sullivan picked it up and handed it to me. "Take that!!" he said, furious.

Why is he handing me a shot glass? Then I realized he meant for it to be a weapon, handing it to me to defend myself with! I asked him, "What are you talking about, Sullivan?!"

He looked me in the eye and said, "Take it, because it's the only chance I'm gonna give ya!"

I was thinking, *What the hell is going on? I don't have any problems with Sullivan, so why is he angry with me?* I didn't even have any clothes on. I definitely wasn't going to take the shot glass from him. Then suddenly he pounds me across the face with a punch. The blow really shook me because I wasn't expecting it. As I tried to figure out what was happening, he took the bread knife and held it to my throat, forcing my head back into the seat, almost breaking the skin. I was unable to move or it would cut my throat.

He said, "Now...I'm goin' to ask ya some fuckin' questions and I want some fuckin' answers." He then asked me where Tommo lived.

Now it all started to make a little sense. Sullivan had recently had a baby with this woman Mary, who had lived with Tommo and me a couple of years back. The whole time we lived together, Mary was dying to fuck Tommo, but he wasn't interested. He would tease her, even let her sleep in the bed with him, but never touch her. She was also a real garbage can for drugs, and Tommo dealt a lot to her, usually on tick. Mary rarely paid him, and recently, Tommo had fallen on hard times. He'd started calling her, asking for money, not threatening her or anything, just pestering. I remembered that a week earlier, Tommo and I were walking down the street, and we stopped so I could light myself a cigarette, and one for him too. Sullivan and Mary were on the opposite side of the street, and Mary was staring at Tommo. Maybe she resented not getting laid, or maybe she was tired of owing Tommo money and said something later to Sullivan. Or maybe Sullivan could see she was giving Tommo the evil eye, who knows, but whatever happened, something got Sullivan amped up and looking for Tommo—and thinking I could tell where to find him.

Tommo lived on Manor Street in Dublin to be exact, but there was no way I was going to give him up to Sullivan. He was my friend and I was loyal to him. Sullivan punched me and punched me, but I wasn't going to rat. All I could do was try to hold up my arms as much as possible, to protect my face and head as best I could. He thumped me again and again and again. I went down on the floor, and Sullivan and Scarecrow stomped on me and kicked me, booted me over and over. Dan didn't take part in the kicking. They picked me up off the floor and put me back in the chair with the knife to my throat. Then more of the same. This shit went on for about a fucking half hour. Sullivan asked me more questions about Tommo and if he had any connections to the IRA, clearly trying to get it square in his own mind whether it was safe for him to touch Tommo because of this. Tommo had family connections and did some things for his locals, but I wasn't telling him that either. Sullivan then started making threats to rape my sister, then threatened to rape Tommo too. I still remember the look on Dan's face after hearing that one. Sullivan was really unhinged.

After a half hour of receiving punches and kicks and the knife to my neck, my face and head had become swollen. It was one of the worst beatings I had ever gotten. Sullivan started wheezing. He was exhausted from beating the shit out of me. Plus, he was clearly on something. The situation was so fucked up, I remember thinking that he might have a heart attack. Then Sullivan just sat down on the coffee table in front of me. There was silence as he put the knife down. And then Sullivan started to explain that Mary told him Tommo threatened to kidnap their child.

That fucking lying bitch. I knew it. I just stared at Sullivan, not knowing what was coming next.

Sullivan lit up a cigarette. He took a drag, quietly looking at me. "When I saw you lightin' that cigarette for Tommo, I knew you were on his side." He calmly leaned forward, looked me in the eye, and said, "Richie, you're a nice fella, but yer fuckin' stupid." As soon as he said that, he jumped forward and bit me on the nose, as hard as he could, like a mad dog. I screamed and tried to get him off me. He was trying to bite the top of my nose off!

The bite didn't just freak me out—even Dan and Scarecrow were horrified. My blood was dripping from Sullivan's mouth. He casually stood up, wiped it, still smoking his cigarette, and told them, "Come on." And they left.

It made no sense. But a lot about gangsters and drug traffickers doesn't quite make sense. I slowly got up, made my way unsteadily to the bathroom, and forced myself to look in the mirror. My nose was still there, but it had bloody teeth marks on it. My face was swollen so much I didn't recognize myself. The feeling was total shock and disbelief. First call was to Tommo to give him the heads-up, then the second was to my friend Ross to take me to the hospital.

To make a long story short, the main outcome of Sullivan and Tommo's feud was me getting my ass kicked. And years later, a chance for me to do a little method acting.

After we shot a few takes of my scene, Weston came up and said, "You nailed it! It felt so real!!" I suppose that shit telegraphs. His instincts had been really good in casting me in that role. Playing the scene had a sort of familiarity, like an inside joke that only I knew.

But I had this bad feeling. I had just nailed my first acting job, and felt like I might have found a path forward, the future I had been searching for. So why wasn't I happier?

I should have learned by this point to listen to Bernard and follow the steps faithfully, but I hadn't. I didn't want to sponsor anyone because it made me uncomfortable, and I didn't feel like my own life was in order enough yet to be telling anyone else how to live theirs. What if I fucked up and told them the wrong thing? They could drink again and it would be all my fault. The stakes for this shit were high. People can die on relapses.

I was still focused on the problems in my own life, not someone else's. And there were plenty of them! Health problems, legal problems, money problems, and marriage problems...I had come so far but I was failing to see that I was still looking inward, instead of outward. And because of that, I just couldn't get excited about the future.

At the time, one of my commitments at the meetings was to sell the literature. Basically, you take care of all the books that are for sale and if anybody who's new wants to buy one, you sell it to them and get more books. The thing with that job is that nobody ever buys any fucking books. It's one of those shitty jobs; maybe you might sell one a year. One evening, I was at my regular meeting, doing my shitty "literature commitment," and in walked Kevin, who was the brother of my old friend, Crazy PJ. Kevin's attendance was on a court card, the old "nudge from the judge" mandating he attend a fixed number of meetings in lieu of going to jail. He knew that I was no lightweight and saw that I was really trying to stay sober, despite my recent misfortunes. He asked if I would be his sponsor and try to help him stay sober.

I remember thinking, *No way, find someone else, I just can't handle this right now*, but I also knew I couldn't turn my back on someone I knew who wanted help, so I agreed. I started taking him to meetings and gave it everything trying to help him. It turned out he had a roommate, Sean, who was also fucked up on drugs.

Sean started coming too, and he asked me to sponsor him as well. All of a sudden, I was responsible for sponsoring these two roommates. I started meeting up with them and teaching them the same stuff Bernard taught me. Answered their calls and tried to advise them as best I could, even though I wasn't at my best. These guys were keeping my mind off my injury and money troubles. I would also be a total hypocrite if I was telling these guys to trust a higher power if I didn't trust mine. *Whatever will be will be...*

It didn't help that Kevin and Sean kept relapsing, smoking weed again and again. Every time they fucked up I would get really down on myself, like it was my fault. Something else to feel bad about. *Maybe I told them the wrong information. Maybe I'm not smart enough to tell them what's right.* I went to Bernard with these questions: Did I tell them the right thing? Am I sponsoring wrong? Am I doing it bad? This kind of shit. Bernard basically told me that I'm not able to keep *anybody* sober. Not even myself. My higher power has to do that. He said all I have to do is answer the phone when they call and teach them the best way that I know how. The rest is up to them and God.

I kept at it, and worked even harder trying to be a good example, coming up with new ways to keep them on the right path. It shouldn't have been a surprise to me, but with all the effort and concentration I was devoting to help them, I found it was impossible to feel sorry for myself. Instead, I focused on putting into practice everything I had learned—having faith in my higher power, looking outward, and being honest with myself and everyone around me.

I had originally started drinking to get out of my own head, but I now noticed something interesting: "being in my own head" felt very different. It wasn't such a bad place to be. That restless, irritable, discontented baseline I used to work from was gone. My level of serenity was usually relative to the amount of effort I put into my program on a daily basis. If I slacked on the work, I felt it. But by helping Kevin and Sean, and adhering to the teachings of the other steps, I usually found myself in a good place mentally. I didn't feel like "Buddha" or anything—I still had issues everyone had—but I could deal with them in a healthy way.

I had completed the twelve steps. There was no graduation. No "Been there, done that, bought the T-shirt." In many ways, my life was still a mess—broken back, broke in the bank, not sure what my future held. But I now had the tools to think clearly. I was taking my points and the goals would come. Like a Gaelic football game, taking the small victories and working for the bigger ones. With my newfound clarity, it was time to make some decisions and take back control of my life. I knew exactly what I wanted to do—I wanted to be an actor. I had found a new career, something I enjoyed that seemed to come natural to me. I was excited by the prospect. The future looked promising.

I moved to Los Angeles and did the usual broke-ass actor jobs like waiting tables, carrying luggage, and driving Uber. Ultimately, I decided to get back into construction, figuring I still had the knowledge to run projects and wouldn't need to lift heavy stuff. The auditions I was sent out on improved, and the roles I landed started getting bigger and better. And I kept going to meetings. Because the twelve steps are a lifelong thing.

In LA meetings I was usually the youngest person, and quite often the only Paddy. That left me fairly self-conscious. I was told that as someone who had completed the twelve steps, I needed to share my story to help the new people, to show them that the program really works. This made me uneasy. I had gotten used to sharing at meetings, but I was reluctant to get up in front of everyone and be The Speaker. And even though I was now acting, often on a crowded set, being honest in front of people is a lot more intimidating than playing a character on film. If you can act, you're only portraying the writing, however good or bad that is, but when you tell your story to a group, the material is your life. And I felt ashamed of a lot of the things I had done, so I wasn't very eager to come clean about my past. Telling Bernard was one thing, but most of the shit you hear at meetings isn't as extreme as what I had been through. You might hear a soccer mom who got a DUI or a guy who hit bottom when he got fired for drinking on the job. I knew, though, that there was no way I was going to refuse to speak.

The night came when I was to tell my story to everyone. I was nervous as hell. I started telling some of the stories that had caused me to hit rock bottom and seek help, but I couldn't even make eye contact with the group I was so worried about their reaction. But I couldn't block out the sound I started to hear...laughter. Not the snarky laughter I experienced with the Ass in a Bag goth douchebags, but genuine "Holy shit, you didn't?!" laughter.

I had been expecting people to listen in horror, but this was anything but that. I hadn't really comprehended the absurdity of what had happened to me until I began telling people at a group level. The stories of kidnapping and drug dealing weren't making them get up and leave like I thought they might. People seemed to be not only entertained by but also appreciative of my story. Intellectually, I knew I was supposed to relate my experiences to help people, but it wasn't until I actually did it that I could understand why.

My story had a happy ending. I wasn't doing these bad things anymore and I was trying to live a positive life.

After I spoke that first time, people in the crowd asked me to speak at their other meetings too. This was not what I had been expecting, but I agreed. Each time I went somewhere I got invited again by someone else. I think I must have spoken at twenty different meetings that year. I began to get more confident, but more importantly, I was living Step Twelve. I was giving it away so I could keep it, so I could stay sober.

I usually ended my talks the same way—the same way I want to end this story—by telling people that I don't pretend to have the answers. This is just a record of the crazy shit that happened to me. I did not invent the steps. They've been around since the 1930s. The twelve steps are the same for every recovery program. There is a tradition of anonymity, so I don't mention the names of the twelve-step programs I'm in out of respect for that, but they are all the same, and they all work.

As of this writing, I have been eleven years sober. I know I'm one of the lucky ones. I have a lot of dead friends. The realization that I was blessed with a second chance is never far from my thoughts, and I want others to have that second chance as well. That is the point of this journey we are on—you are never in it alone, and to stay on track you help others get on track.

You might be wondering what happened to the rest of my old gangs. Some are dead. One of them owns a few Airbnbs in Dublin. One manages a supermarket. One is CFO of some tech companies. One is the principal of a high school. And one of us is an actor in Hollywood. You can guess which. I know that most of them wouldn't like me revealing their identities.

I don't worry too much about what will be anymore—maybe because I have come through so much craziness already. I don't feel like killing myself these days, and I don't need to take drugs or drink to live life. It's because of the people that helped save my life. They showed me the tools from the twelve steps and a different way to live. It's easier to stay positive and look at my world with hope. Besides, a different quote seems much more appropriate to my life now, this one from one of Ireland's greatest ne'er-do-wells, Oscar Wilde: "The only difference between the saint and the sinner is that every saint has a past, and every sinner has a future."

ACKNOWLEDGMENTS

Richie:

John and Dave for answering my email and taking a chance on me.

All of my sponsors for taking the time to help me in recovery.

The recovery groups in San Francisco who welcomed me and
put up with my shit. Especially Sunset Sobriety. Shamrocks and
Serenity, Sometimes Slowly, The Trudgers and The Lads.

My family for putting up with the drama I brought.

Vanessa for being such an awesome manager.

Jacob for some wonderful editing and input.

The folks at Post Hill.

Jan, Lacy, and the folks at Dupree Miller.

Nick and Ben for the encouragement.

And Elaine. This is *your* Playground Moment.

John and Dave:

Would like to thank their wives, Leah and Jenn.

Jan Miller and Lacy Lynch at Dupree Miller and
Associates for making this book a reality.

Jacob Hoye for helping push it across the finish line.

Thanks to Jake Steinfeld for believing in this
project and always believing in us.

And, of course, we are grateful to Richie for opening his life to us.

ABOUT THE AUTHORS

RICHIE STEPHENS is an irish actor and writer who lives in Los Angeles, California. He is best known for playing villains in films and on TV, including *Blue Bloods, MacGyver, Criminal Minds,* and *Days of Our Lives,* his appearances in multiple Florence + the Machine music videos, and his ability to do a broad range of accents. He has appeared in over one hundred stage and screen productions, and is a member of Oscar-winner Bobby Moresco's Actor's Gym—an exclusive group of working actors and writers. He's also been a circuit speaker in recovery groups, and he actively works with the homeless at The Midnight Mission and The Center in Hollywood. You can find him at www.richiestephens.com and @richieactor on Instagram and twitter.

JOHN ALTSCHULER and DAVE KRINSKY are screenwriters who co-created and executive produced the Emmy Award-winning show *Silicon Valley.* They were also Executive Producers of the Emmy Award-winning show *King of the Hill* and wrote the hit comedy movie *Blades of Glory* starring Will Ferrell. They met at the University of North Carolina at Chapel Hill, where they created the first student-produced comedy show on UNC Student Television, then wrote for the legendary humor magazine *National Lampoon,* before moving to Los Angeles. In addition to several Emmy nominations, they received a SXSW film award for their work on *Silicon Valley,* and have also won an Environmental Media Award.